SOCIETY & THE VICTORIANS

DEMOCRACY AND REACTION

SOCIETY & THE VICTORIANS
General Editors : John Spiers
and Cecil Ballantine

The Harvester Press series 'Society & the Victorians'
makes available again important works by and about
the Victorians. Each of the titles chosen has been
either out of print and difficult to find, or ex-
ceedingly rare for many years. A few titles, although
available in the secondhand market, are needed in
modern critical editions and the series attempts
to meet this demand.

Scholars of established reputation **provide** substantial introductions, and the **majority of** titles
have textual notes and a full bibliography. Texts
are reprinted from the best editions.

Democracy and Reaction

by L. T. Hobhouse

Edited with introduction and notes

by P. F. Clarke
Lecturer in History, University College, London

THE HARVESTER PRESS 1972

THE HARVESTER PRESS
Publishers

50 Grand Parade
Brighton Sussex
BN2 2QA
England

'Democracy and Reaction' first published
in 1904 by T. Fisher Unwin, London
This edition first published in 1972
'Society & The Victorians' number three

'Democracy and Reaction' 1904 and 1909
© Executors of the estate of the late L.T. Hobhouse

Introduction and notes © P.F. Clarke 1972

LC Card No. 78–168941
ISBN 0 901759 72 4

Printed in England by Redwood Press Limited
Trowbridge, Wiltshire

Contents

Note on the Text

The text of *Democracy and Reaction* printed here is that of the first edition (published in 1904). This has been preferred to that of the second edition of 1909 in order to preserve the original emphasis of the work. The textual changes were in any case minor, and attention is drawn to the more significant of them in the notes; the main difference between the two editions was the addition of a new introduction which is reprinted here as an appendix. But it is worth recovering the 1904 text because Hobhouse's message, or at least the form in which he delivered it, was intimately conditioned by the circumstances of the time. As I argue in my introduction, the shape of the work underwent an important transformation between its serial publication in 1901-2 and its appearance as a book in 1904. I have shown in detail in the textual notes how the thrust of Hobhouse's argument was modified. The Cobdenite revivalism of 1904 represented a different political climate from the imperialistic euphoria of 1901; the unfolding of progressive Liberalism by 1909 marked a further phase. Many of Hobhouse's arguments have a permanent significance; but it is the contemporary overtones and references of the first edition which best capture the particular context in which they were mounted.

I should like to thank my colleague, Dr. J.A. Thompson, for his help in preparing this edition.

P.F.C.

Introduction

The issue of the left-wing Liberal weekly, the *Speaker*, for 7 December 1901 contained the last of six articles by J.A. Hobson on Imperialism (his book, *Imperialism, A Study* was to be published in the following year). Hobson's theoretical work on these lines — greatly influential as it has been throughout the rest of the century — grew out of the specific events of the war which Britain had been waging against the Boer republics since 1899. *Democracy and Reaction* has achieved less fame. Yet it is appropriate that Hobson's series of articles should have been succeeded in the *Speaker* the following week by a contribution from his friend, L.T. Hobhouse; and the eight articles, of which that was the first, represent the genesis of the present book. Like Hobson, Hobhouse saw in the South African War a manifestation of deep-seated malignant developments at home in Britain.[1] Unlike Hobson, Hobhouse preferred to base his political analysis on social and intellectual, rather than economic, trends. The need for some kind of quasi-historical stock-taking, however, was felt in broadly similar terms by both men; and both sought to develop a more general critique from the particular predicament with which they were confronted. *Democracy and Reaction*, like much of Hobhouse's work, is at present generally undervalued; but, along with his justly famous book on *Liberalism* and his important study of *Social Evolution and Political Theory*, it presents the mature achievement of a political thinker whom Hobson called "one of the less known of the great men of our time."[2] The problems confronted here, moreover, are ones which men of a progressive outlook in later generations have ignored only at their peril.

Hobhouse's first article posed the questions which he felt impelled to ask and, if possible, answer. They were, he claimed, "root questions", and that because "a great upheaval takes us back to root questions." The tone is that of fundamental reappraisal. "Two short years," he wrote, "have sufficed to shatter many illusions." (The article is entitled 'Some shattered illusions'.) What the War had accomplished more plainly than anything else was to suggest "a certain scepticism as to the reality of civilised progress." It is less the barbarity of war itself than the acquiescence in barbarity by the democracy – a "deterioration of public opinion" – which is the 'root' of Hobhouse's inquiry. If Hobhouse had been merely a lily-livered Liberal, disillusioned with the masses, his arguments would be of rather less interest and pertinence than in fact they are. In the book of 1904, however, even more clearly than in the articles of 1901-2, Hobhouse moves beyond the shattered illusions. This is illustrated literally in the present title, where 'Democracy' and 'Reaction' turn out to be, not partners in crime, but the Jekyll and Hyde of British politics. That Hobhouse should in this instance seek to redefine the idea of progress rather than abandon it, is wholly characteristic. He was the revisionist *par excellence:* girding old truths in new armour. Indeed his life-work can be seen as a subtle and persistent effort to reconcile the best of the old and the new – not only in political theory but in philosophy and sociology – rather than allow useful energies to be diffused through needless conflict.

II

Hobhouse was forty when *Democracy and Reaction* was published: He came from an old landowning family in the west country; his father was a clergyman of the Church of England; he was educated at Marlborough and at Corpus Christi College, Oxford. His son recalled that "Father was immensely conservative in some ways, and would not take up with a reversal of the old order of things." [3] A traditionalist, then, up to a point – but up to a point only. For we find him even in school debates invoking Mazzini in defence of democracy, and at Corpus carrying an anti-monarchical motion in the college debating society. He was to stay on at Corpus as a don teaching philosophy. By the late 1880s, at which time he was espousing the cause of the New Unions, he could be described as a 'socialist'. His first book, *The Labour Movement* (1893), was a sympathetic examination of the forces making for collectivist solutions to social and industrial problems. But the advanced nature of his thinking did not cut him off from Liberalism: at least, not Liberalism as understood by the *Manchester Guardian,* which was in the 1890s entering upon its great phase under the editorship of C.P. Scott. "All that there is, or is to come, in the opening out of the human mind is Liberalism," wrote Hobhouse later, "and it was in this sense that Scott understood it." [4] Late in 1896 Scott, another old Corpus man, invited Hobhouse to join the paper; and the connexion then established was to be finally severed only by death.

Now there can be no doubt that Hobhouse was in many ways happy to be grappling with live political issues as a leader writer in Manchester — "I was in my right milieu there as I have never been before or since," he once recalled [5] — but journalism never became his whole life. In the mornings he continued his studies in philosophy (by now perhaps more properly called sociology) and only later in the day did he go to Cross Street. His book *Mind in Evolution* was published in 1901, and *Morals in Evolution* was to follow in 1906. Throughout his life Hobhouse managed to combine serious academic work in large and important fields with writings of a more general character on political and social subjects. "Hobhouse is working, of course, in his usual steam-engine style," is a comment on the undergraduate. It rings true too of the journalist, who would "write in one evening the long leader and the two 'shorts' before the rest of us had fairly got going." [6] This quickness of mind and facility with the pen enabled Hobhouse to maintain his double interests. The gain was the robust practicality he brought to his scholarship and the impressive erudition he brought to his polemical writings. There was a price to pay. "He wrote 'as it came'; and it came too easily." [7] This is perhaps a severe judgment; but in reading a book like *Democracy and Reaction* one is sometimes conscious that Hobhouse did not linger over his text. On the other hand, the ideas he is expressing are by no means fugitive. He is a systematic thinker. The arguments in his various works are consistent; they support and illuminate each other. And references, especially to his lesser-known writings, will be so employed here.

The *Manchester Guardian* opposed the Boer War, not only

in prospect, but after the outbreak of hostilities too. In terms of day-to-day politics Scott and Hobhouse found that the War did little to enhance their admiration for the leaders of the Liberal party. Campbell-Bannerman (for whom they came to feel a posthumous affection) they regarded for years as a "feeble" leader with "no backbone". His colleagues seemed to have "neither a mind nor a will nor a democratic principle among them". [8] The chastisement on pp. 129-30 of those who argued "we ought never to have started, but having started we cannot go back", is the faint echo of this revulsion. The only leading Liberal who came anywhere near living up to Hobhouse's expectations was John Morley, who, steeped in the tradition of Cobden and Gladstone, had the inclination if not the will to lead a peace movement. Hobhouse could respect this. He hoped indeed that Morley might join to his 'Radical' critique of foreign policy that 'progressive' outlook on social policy which Hobhouse saw as a logical corollary. Morley would not move so far. But, at any rate, as an anti-imperialist Hobhouse found himself in the same boat, not only with Labour men, but with Gladstonian die-hards who opposed socialism root and branch; whereas those Liberal Imperialists who had supported the progressive position — Haldane had written the preface for *The Labour Movement* — were now divided from him on the first issue of the day.

Early in 1901 we find Hobhouse telling Scott of his wish to leave the *Guardian,* and advancing as a reason his difficulty in writing for a Liberal paper at a time when "unless some great & unforeseen change occurs the Liberal party seems to me destined to futility . . ." [9] This mood of disillusion was real enough and is to be detected a few months later in the articles he wrote for the *Speaker* while still on the staff of the *Guardian.* But what ultimately weighed with Hobhouse in forsaking Manchester was the impossibility, even for him, of permanently maintaining his double work when he felt philosophy as the first call. In 1902 he moved to London. In 1904 *Democracy and Reaction* appeared. In 1907, following unsatisfactory spells of political and journalistic work, Hobhouse became the first Martin White Professor of Sociology at the London School of Economics, and he held this chair for the rest of his life.

INTRODUCTION

Democracy and Reaction, then, belongs in origin to the last part of Hobhouse's period with the *Guardian*; though the final form of the book reflects his pursuit of more sustained academic activities. It is interesting to trace the way in which Hobhouse made the articles of 1901-2 into the book of 1904. The structure of the two directly corresponds in the following way:

Speaker articles (14 Dec. 1901 - 8 Feb. 1902)	*Democracy and Reaction*
1. Some shattered illusions	pp. 70-2: part of ch.iii
2. The limitations of democracy	pp. 139-47)
3. Democracy and liberty	pp. 147-57) ch. vi
4. Democracy and nationality	pp. 157-64)
5. Democracy and imperialism	pp. 16-29 (much expanded), 47-8: ch. ii
6. The growth of imperialism	pp. 168-77: part of ch.vii
7. The intellectual reaction	pp. 57-62, 84-7) ch. iii
8. The intellectual reaction	pp. 77-80, 63-7)

In the *Speaker* Hobhouse began with the shattered illusions about democracy [1] and went on to examine how democracy had dealt with Liberal ideas [2,3,4]; it then appeared that the growth of Imperialism [5] was not peculiarly the responsibility of democracy [6] but, on the contrary, was put down to the influence of Social Darwinism [7] and Idealist philosophy [8] on a middle class predisposed to conservatism. This is rather like a whodunit. Imperialism is the crime; democracy is the obvious suspect which, in the best tradition, is acquitted after a fair number of red herrings have been disposed of. *Democracy and Reaction* is constructed in a different way. Here the problem is set up in basically historical terms (chs. i and ii), taking the *Speaker's* final *dénouement* as read (ch. iii). The analysis is then elaborated with material drawing on *Mind in Evolution* (ch. iv) and *Morals in Evolution* (ch. v). The book finally moves to an appraisal of the future value of the ideas of Liberalism (ch. vi), of democracy (ch. vii), and of the Gladstonian ethic (ch. viii), concluding with a discussion of the relation of socialism to Liberalism (ch. ix). The result of these changes is to modify the thrust of the argument in one important respect. In the *Speaker* Hobhouse asked, *given* Liberal ideas can democracy be justified? In

Democracy and Reaction the question is, *given* democratic ideas in Liberalism still relevant? [10] The fact that the answer is in both cases affirmative should not be allowed to obscure this difference.

Anyone who, like Hobhouse, was on the wrong side in the Khaki Election of 1900 was not likely to idealise the dispassionate rationality of the British voter. Churchill, who had been on the right side, was able in later years to explain that in 1900 — "before the liquefaction of the British political system had set in" — "we had a real political democracy led by a hierarchy of statesmen, and not a fluid mass distracted by newspapers." [11] Hobhouse, on the other hand, was less impressed by that new vogue figure, "the-man-in-the-street", whom he describes on pp. 70-6. Yet both men's impressions rest on strictly contemporary first-hand acquaintance with the Lancashire working class. If Churchill's view of democracy was volatile, Hobhouse's remained consistently wary. "The mob mind," he wrote in the second edition, "has forgotten everything and learnt nothing, and the danger inherent in the permanent presence of this mass of inflammable material has in no sense passed away." [12]

But it is nonetheless true that the passage of time was an important factor in modifying the terms of Hobhouse's "root questions". When he came to put together *Democracy and Reaction* it seemed clear that in politics the tide had turned. By the time of the second edition in 1909, he was, with hindsight, confident in distinguishing a period of reaction lasting from 1886-1902; and even in 1904 he sensed that "it is not impossible that the year 1903 will be regarded by historians as marking the end, and therefore also the beginning of an era in political thought." (p.3). From the beginning of Chamberlain's Tariff Reform campaign onwards, far from Liberalism meeting undeserved rebuffs, it enjoyed unexampled good fortune. "For four years the Board of Trade figures in their courses fought against Mr. Chamberlain," was how Hobhouse put it in 1909. [13] In these circumstances it was natural that the sceptical Hobhouse should turn his scrutiny from democracy to Liberalism. The whole conditions of the problem had changed. Indeed when he came to incorporate into ch. iii part of the article of 8 February 1902, analysing the plight of

Liberalism in class terms, he included it in its original form as a direct quotation on pp. 63-7: so dated had it already become.

Hobhouse's attitude towards Liberalism was clearly influenced by his attitude towards Imperialism; of his hostility to which little need be added to the indictment he makes in these pages. His personal detestation of the policies and methods of Joseph Chamberlain made him sympathetic to men like Morley who repudiated them. But Morley stood, not for progressivism, but for that old Liberalism which, as Hobhouse confesses on pp. 209-10, he had regarded in the 1890s as outworn and obstructive. However justifiable such a feeling might have been in regard to domestic politics, its bearing on Imperial politics could no longer be ignored. "The socialistic development of Liberalism," Hobhouse admits on p. 12, "paved the way for Imperialism by diminishing the credit of the school which had stood most strictly for the doctrines of liberty, fair dealing, and forbearance in international affairs." The hope some had entertained of combining Imperialism with domestic reform had been exploded by the War (p. 49). It was truer to say of democracy — which for Hobhouse was more a social ideal than an electoral mechanism — that "in embracing Imperialism it has, as the phrase goes, 'contradicted itself'." (p. 167). The necessary connexion between reactionary policies at home and abroad, which Hobhouse repeatedly asseverates, is the basis of his reassessment of the old Liberalism, since "in the new principles we see the whole circle of the Cobdenist ideas turned, as it were, inside out." (p. 55). And similarly it leads him to draw the lesson, "not that the older Liberalism is 'played out', but that the several elements of its doctrines are more vitally connected than appears on the surface." (pp. 164-5).

Now Hobhouse had never been in much danger of throwing over traditional Liberalism entire. But his emphasis on its practical vindication in the test of war reflected a real shift of opinion, and one that was widespread. The improbable combination of progressives, Gladstonians and Labour in opposition to Imperialism led each group towards a more sympathetic understanding of the position of the others. The record which the Cobdenite F.W. Hirst, Morley's secretary, made of a meeting with Hobhouse in August 1899 is, in its way, testimony to this. "His views have changed a good deal since he left Corpus," Hirst noted. "Three years ago at Oxford . . . I felt we were rather far apart in politics. Both of us have moved, but he, I think, the most. He speaks and thinks very differently now of Cobden and Bright." [14] For Hobhouse it was not so much a question of reverting to an old faith which he had mistakenly abandoned as of seeking to justify the essential congruence of progressive politics and Cobdenite principles. As an exercise in persuasion this aimed at leading socialists back towards Liberalism and Liberals on towards socialism.

The spirit in which he approached his task of reconcilation is well illustrated by something he wrote a few years later in a treatment of Locke's view of property. "The conception is individualistic," he admitted, "*but it may be given a more social turn*" – if certain points were borne in mind. [15] Granted the legitimacy of the method, Hobhouse has little difficulty in deriving the new Liberalism from the old, by characterising the differences between them as ones over means not ends. He suggested elsewhere "that the true interpretation of the modern movement is not to be reached by setting up an abstract opposition between state inter-ference on the one hand and the liberty of the individual on the other; the question at stake is as to the kind of liberty which shall be left to the individual and the kind of respon-sibility that falls to the community." And if democratic thinkers now took a different view from that of Cobden and Bright – "It does not follow that they value liberty less, though it may perhaps be true that they trust to government more."[16] And so we find Hobhouse on pp. 212-23 examining the premises of Cobden's individualism, and enlarging the loopholes Cobden himself allowed for state action, to suggest "that the breach of principle between the Liberalism of Cobden's time and the Liberalism of to-day is much smaller than appears on the surface." (p. 219). The explanation Hobhouse advances for the illusion of a breach is important. Because Cobden and Bright "were tempted to generalise their arguments", (which was natural enough), he argues that "the doctrine of popular liberty, which enshrined a social truth of permanent value, became identified with doctrines restricting collective action, which were of merely temporary value." (p. 221).

IV

In explaining the 'intellectual reaction' of the late nineteenth century Hobhouse singles out the influence of Idealist philosophy as a prime target. The harsh terms in which he describes "the effect of idealism on the world in general" on p. 78 are softened a little in the second edition. "Idealism has had its value," he begins there, only to go on to repeat the substance of his charge. His conviction that Idealism must bear responsibility for "discrediting the principles upon which liberal progress has been founded" [17] was unwavering throughout the years. He laid the blame squarely on the complacency induced by what he insisted was a doctrine of the perfection of the world order. "If all that is real is rational," he argued, "it is difficult to resist the view that what wins is right." [18] Hobhouse would not admit that his criticism was in any way vitiated by the Liberal political principles upheld by the most influential of the English Idealists, T.H. Green. "As a teacher and re-former Green himself was thoroughly alive to 'the difference between the ideal and the actual'. Yet his metaphysical theory supplies no adequate explanation of the gulf between them." [19]

Hobhouse's relation to Green is rather complex. On the publication of *Democracy and Reaction* there was some wry comment at finding "one reared in Oxford affirming that the stream of German idealism 'has swelled the current of retrogression'." [20] It is perfectly true that the doctrines associated with Green's name dominated the intellectual climate of Oxford during Hobhouse's time there. But in his own college, under the influences of Thomas Case, a positivist approach was upheld even in the heyday of Idealist metaphysics. And Hobhouse's heterodoxy in this respect has much to do with the dispiriting reception which his *Theory of Knowledge* received in 1896, and hence, perhaps, with his move to Manchester. When in Manchester he finally resolved to devote himself to philosophy once more, it was in the consciousness that "hitherto I have failed, as I am well aware, even to get my work taken seriously." [21] It is in this context that we should appreciate Hobhouse's autobiographical comment that "though attracted by T.H. Green's social and ethical outlook I could not see in his metaphysics a valid philosophical solution." [22] Despite his rejection of these Hegelian modes of reasoning, Hobhouse found much to admire in Green's political theory.

The reason for this is plain; and it recalls his attempt to distinguish the essential from the inessential in Cobden's political thought. In seeking to discredit a particular philosophical system, Hobhouse had no wish to discredit Green. Green himself had professed a reverence for Mill despite their metaphysical differences; and in practical terms Green's politics were not inconsistent with Utilitarian criteria. [23] Hobhouse stands in an analogous relation towards Green. Anticipating that philosophy would turn away from Idealism, he had early resolved to "set his face against Green being treated as Mill had been." [24] And he preferred to consider Green the political thinker in terms of a Liberal tradition which had been carried forward at different times by men of different schools. In his inaugural lecture he was at pains to demonstrate that, like Bentham and Mill before him, Green had "a practical situation in view", to which his theory of contract, of freedom and of the common good was a response. [25] It is in this sense that he describes Green as Mill's "true successor in the line of political thinkers". (p. 224 n.). And in his later years Hobhouse would enter a caveat with his students — "I think you're too hard on T.H. Green. He didn't dare to say too much in those days . . ." [26]

What was the basis of this supposed tradition? On p. 11 Hobhouse approvingly quotes some remarks from Green's lecture on 'Liberal legislation and freedom of contract', arguing for the continuity of Liberalism on the ground that "The same old cause of social good against class interests" underlay its destructive and constructive phases alike. This is, of course, a view of Liberalism directly opposed to that of Herbert Spencer who denounced "this spreading confusion of thought which has led it, in pursuit of what appears to be public good, to invert the method by which in earlier days it achieved public good." [27] In Spencer's view Liberalism was essentially a means; it amounted to little more than *laissez faire*. In Green's view, which Hobhouse considered for all practical purposes reconcilable with Mill's view and his own, Liberalism was characterised by its ends. In Mill these come down to the greatest happiness; in Green to the common good; and in Hobhouse to the principle of harmony. That a possible harmony could be found between the claims of different persons Hobhouse elsewhere called "the fundamental postulate of social ethics"; and he was prepared to regard "the idea of harmony as the touchstone of social development." [28]

Green's principles were of most use to Hobhouse in the 1890s when he concentrated on arguing the collectivist case; conversely, Mill's individualism comes to be treated reverently in *Democracy and Reaction*. On pp. 223-4 Hobhouse prefers Mill on liberty to Green, on the grounds that in Green's conception — as the right of a man to make the best of himself — the vital question of whether a man is to judge for himself is evaded. This is a fair point. But Hobhouse does not appear entirely to resolve the difficulties he recognises here. On pp. 124-5 in his treatment of individual rights Hobhouse is clearly following Green. [29] Thus Green's assertion "that the claim or right of the individual to have certain powers secured to him by society . . . rest(s) on the fact that these powers are necessary to the fulfilment of a man's vocation as a moral being . . ." is taken over almost intact by Hobhouse (possibly becoming more lucid in the process). Indeed in the footnote on p. 125 he elaborates on the limitation, "as a moral being", glossing it to mean compatible with social harmony. This is certainly consistent with the brusque treatment in *The Labour Movement:* "If, therefore, any right to any form of property or freedom no longer serves a good social purpose, it must go." [30] And the more sophisticated discussion in ch. vi of *Liberalism* has the same tendency. But what seems rather to have been lost sight of is the admitted superiority of Mill's defence of a man's "right to make his own mistakes."

V

With the examination of evolution and sociology we enter another area in which Hobhouse brought his academic expertise to bear. The burden of his charge is that what I

shall call for convenience 'Social Darwinism' was sociologically naive — "we do not find that it is based on the science
of society," he writes on p. 96. The line of criticism which
he adopts is not peculiarly his own — it probably owes
something to the American sociologist Lester Ward [31] —
but the cogency with which it is developed is testimony
to his sustained concern with these problems. Because of
its lack of a grounding in sociology. Social Darwinism
relied on the application from biology of 'laws of evolution'
which underestimated the evolutionary role of intelligence
and social traditions. Hence it overlooked the rise of ethical
systems under which "the conception of duty becomes remodelled on the basis of a rational understanding of the
actual needs of individual and social life." (p. 107). Hobhouse argued from history that the stage of haphazard
development had been succeeded by a stage dominated
by mind, enabling society to be consciously organised in
terms of order and liberty. This process involved "the
progressive curtailment of the struggle for existence" in
the interests of social justice. "Hence," as Hobhouse puts it
in his inaugural lecture, "the more closely actual institutions conform to the requirements of social justice the
more likely are they to bring to the top the man best
fitted to save society."[32] In this way he tried to hoist
Social Darwinism with its own petard and to show that
the application of a social ethic was required by evolution
itself.

It is in the application of this view that he will write
confidently on p. 127, "this is the line of progress"; or on
p. 226 of "the problem of progress, or what is the same
thing, social justice." So far, so good. But in annexing
progress to the social developments he found desirable,
has Hobhouse proved too much? Harold Laski argues that
both he and Green were guilty here: "Given goodwill, they
tended to believe that history made itself, and beneficently,
if it was only left alone." [33] Now part of his charge ("they
did not see that we have deliberately to create the common
good by building the necessary institutions and processes
through which it becomes possible") is clearly countered
by the argument in the inaugural lecture quoted above.
More broadly, one can confute it by pointing to other
explicit statements — the comment on p. 94 that "by the

conception of destiny the moral consciousness is paralysed";
or the flat assertion in Hobhouse's later study of social
evolution: "The theory of continuous automatic inevitable
progress is impossible." [34] Because men were in a position
to exert conscious control over their social arrangements a
measure of choice was at each stage open to them. Society
might retrogress. Or, if a wrong alternative were chosen,
development (defined in terms of social organisation) would
not represent progress (defined in terms of social justice).

Notwithstanding these theoretical possibilities, Hobhouse
makes many efforts at proving a broad empirical correlation
between ethical progress and social development. "But
why?" asks J.W.Burrows. "What good will it do him?" [35]
This was a question posed, almost in so many words, by
Hobhouse himself. [36] The answer he suggested has a bearing
on Burrow's further observation that a modern sociologist
or political theorist, however committed, would only require that their "proposed programme should be sociologically *possible.*" Perhaps Hobhouse's requirement is not very
different. In one of his works he actually quotes the dictum
that the ethically right must be sociologically possible. [37]
And the manner of his explicit reply is similar: "The study
of actual evolution in the past does not suffice to tell us
with certainty either what ought to be or what will be, but
it tells us what may be." [38] It ought to be added that, at a
time when sociology was seen primarily in evolutionary
terms, this was to furnish very helpful letters of credit.

Furthermore, although the claim to predict the future
was, strictly speaking, never essential to Hobhouse's case,
his conclusion that in the long run development was progressive was clearly important to him. This was not because
of a callow optimism. Rather, he was himself pessimistic
by temperament. And his own political convictions were
not usually those in the ascendant (his adult political life
lasted from 1885-1928, years which saw a strong progressive
Government only from 1906-14). Churchill once wrote of
Morley: "He had had too long experience of defeat to
nourish a sanguine hope." [39] Hobhouse was in a like
position. For him the idea of progress was the bright light
in an immediately discouraging world. The struggle in his
mind between a fatalistic view of events and a faith in the
efficacy of rational ideas is vividly expressed in a passage,

too long to quote here, printed in the *Memoir*. [40] Moreover, it should by now be apparent that Hobhouse's correlation of progress and evolution does not show that, given
the developed, he can find it good. Instead it finds him
affirming that what we know on other grounds to be good
is also more developed than what we know to be bad. And
from this he drew the corollary: "The failures are the un-
developed, and if you would know what development can
do you must look at its successes." [41]

VI

Hobhouse's hopes for social progress, then, rested on
the possibilities of applying ethical principles to political
relations. This opened the way to a large degree of collective
responsibility. The view of property taken on pp. 230-2
holds it to be justified only by social service. In respect of
the existing industrial system, therefore, it prompts proposals
for remedial measures of appropriation and public ownership. We find that there are only differences of tone in
Hobhouse's treatment of this important topic from the
1890s to the 1920s. In *The Labour Movement* (1893) he is
scathing about "the forces of Private Enterprise and Free
Competition." [42] The analysis in *Liberalism* (1911) is an
elaboration of that in the present work. Perhaps the discussion which gives the clearest idea of his position is in
the essay he contributed to a collection published in 1913,
mainly by High Church disciples of T.H. Green. There he
distinguishes the conception of property for use from that
of property for power; and points to the prevalence of the
latter in modern capitalism. "The rise of large-scale industry,"
he infers, "has abolished the possibility of any form of
individualism as a general solution of the economic problem." [43] The answer he suggests here is to allow property
for use to the individual but to reserve the disposal of
property for power to the democratic state.

The practical steps towards such an end which had been
envisaged in the 1890s are enumerated on pp. 50-1. In *The
Labour Movement* we find the state lauded as "the supreme
regulative authority", free of the sectional interests dominating lesser communities and therefore able to harmonise
them. The judgment of the democratic state is "the nearest

approach to a collective judgment of the social organism
upon its collective interests, parallel to the judgment of the
individual man on his private interests." [44] A broad measure
of collectivism was justified on this basis. But only on this
basis. In one of the most interesting leaders Hobhouse
wrote for the *Guardian* he urged that "there is all the
difference between benevolent officialism setting the world
in order from above, and the democratic Collectivism which
seeks not to restrict liberty but to fulfil it." [45] On pp. 221-2
we find the positive role of the state defended on the
grounds of the moral obligation felt by a self-governing
community towards its members. Without democracy the
case was different. As Hobhouse put it in a pamphlet of
1910, "the extension of public responsibility under a representative system is one thing; under any other system it is
open to quite another set of objections." [46]

Of the nature of these objections *Democracy and Reaction* should leave the reader in no doubt. That Hobhouse
should have become more overtly antibureaucratic (as
Hirst noted he had in 1899) [47] was no doubt bound up
with his attitude in British policy in South Africa, where,
he was able to write in the second edition, "bureaucracy
had failed". [48] Hobhouse comments on p. 169 that there
is no reason for thinking that the corruption of public
opinion "would be corrected by a government of select
Balliol men." Milner is clearly one target, here, as he is in
the ironical treatment of the 'expert' on p. 120. But in
mounting these objections Hobhouse also had the Fabians
in mind. The Fabians, of course, had gone wrong in imagin-
ing that socialism was compatible with Imperialism. The
type of socialist we encounter on p. 159, who "amuses
himself with the belief that he can 'organise' the great
capitalists for his own purposes", was originally explicitly
a Fabian. [49] Hobhouse's attitude toward the Webbs was
ambivalent. Sidney Webb he described in 1890 as "one of
the most interesting men I have ever met."[50] But the
Webbs' vision of achieving socialism by stealth as the
collectivist state spread its tentacles was not congenial to
him. The sort of socialism which attracted Hobhouse implied
a rectification of "moral damage" through a "change of
spirit". "If the change from individualism to socialism
means nothing but an alteration in the methods of organising

industry," he wrote in 1893, "it would leave the nation no happier or better than before." [51] The Fabian reaction to events in South Africa confirmed his doubts. He concurred with Scott's view that it was "sad about the Webbs" — "They have been raking about among statistics too long." [52] Hence on pp. 227-9 we find the deprecation of a "distortion" of socialism (clearly Fabian) under which: "Everything is to fall into the hands of an 'expert', who will sit in an office and direct the course of the world, prescribing to men and women precisely how they are to be virtuous and happy."

Towards Labour and socialism in their more common form, however, Hobhouse's attitude is quite different. As he had written in 1889, the relations of Liberalism and Labour had been impaired. "But between these two forces, union is at bottom natural and in the end necessary." [53] And these were the forces which anti-imperialism had brought together. Since socialistic legislation, on his showing, "comes not to destroy but to fulfil" the ideals of Liberalism (p. 217), while "the true Socialism is avowedly based on the political victories which Liberalism won" (p. 229), the differences between the two ought to disappear. It was his lifelong belief that "if we divided parties by true principles", ordinary Labour and good Liberal stood together. [54] This grouping was at the heart of the Edwardian progressive movement. And it was electorally successful, in that it dominated British politics from 1906 until the Great War, thus giving Hobhouse real grounds for hope. Equally, he also felt moved to dwell in the second edition on the difficulties of keeping "the easily estranged forces of thin-skinned and irritable idealists" in a working combination. [55] But as evidence of their ideological compatibility he added a footnote to ch. ix remarking "that during the present Parliament such controversies as have arisen between official Liberalism and Labour have as often turned on consistency in applying Liberal principles as on divergences of aim between Liberalism and Socialism." [56]

Hobhouse's assessment of the prospects for social democracy in the early twentieth century is the final theme of the book. He does not minimise the inherent weaknesses of democracy as a form of government. On pp. 146-7 he suggests that knowledge necessarily limits democratic

control, and on pp. 182-3 points to the feeling of impotence
and remoteness which the individual voter feels. But the
main obstacle is one he sees in simpler terms. In 1897 he
set forth the view that: "The power of organised capital
is the standing danger of democracy." [57] He never modified
it. On pp. 237-8 he describes the political influence of
wealth in the same terms, and his identification of the
House of Lords and the Press as its chief agents is endorsed
in the preface to the second edition. Insofar as the reactionary elements were united, they were able to mount
successive onslaughts in different fields; the effect, however,
was successively to arouse the hostility of those threatened.
The shape of the progressive movement was hammered out
on the anvil of adversity. To impart his vision of the need
for unity among progressives in the face of united opponents
was not the least of Hobhouse's ambitions.

Hobhouse did not find much of substance to amend when
a second edition was published in 1909. In his new introduction he sought to broaden the application of his arguments. The "awakening of the East" led him to confront
the question of racial equality which, by and large, he begs
in this edition. "It is conceivable, after all," he concluded,
"that to our grandchildren the world will present itself,
not as a white oligarchy, ruling and exploiting millions of
yellow, brown, and black, but as a system of self-governing
peoples linked by mutual respect and international agree-
ment rather than by bonds of authority and subordination." [58] Otherwise his message remained unchanged. It would
appear to be that edition of the book which fell into the
hands of a young working-class man from Warrington, who
wrote later that it "introduced me, so to speak, to a new
world of thought". [59] And it is more generally true that, as
in the experience of that reader, *Democracy and Reaction*
constitutes a fitting introduction to Hobhouse's great work
Liberalism which followed in 1911.

Notes

1. Not only is Hobson cited on p.30 below, but the argument developed on p.66, as originally printed in the *Speaker*, included a reference to Hobson's demonstration of the role of finance capital.

2. J.A. Hobson and Morris Ginsberg, *L.T. Hobhouse, his life and work* (1931) (hereafter cited as *Memoir*), p.72.

3. *Memoir*, p.90.

4. *C.P. Scott, 1846-1932. The making of the 'Manchester Guardian'* (1946), p.84.

5. Hobhouse to Scott, 19 April 1907. All letters quoted are from the C.P. Scott papers in the possession of the *Guardian*, on which I draw throughout this section.

6. *Memoir*, pp.18, 83.

7. Ernest Barker, 'Leonard Trelawney Hobhouse', *Proceedings of The British Academy,* xv (1931), p.16.

8. Hobhouse to Scott, 7 April 1899; cf. Hobhouse to Scott, 25 Feb. 1899, and Scott to Hobhouse, 23 Jan. 1902. On this phase of Hobhouse's life see P.F. Clarke, *Lancashire and the New Liberalism* (Cambridge, 1971), ch.7, sections iv-vii.

9. Hobhouse to Scott, 14 Feb. 1901.

10. This is true *a fortiori* of the second edition (1909).

11. W.S. Churchill, *My Early Life* (1930; Fontana edn. 1959), p.365.

12. Introduction to second edition, p.xli.

13. Ibid., p.xiii.

14. F.W. Hirst, *In the Golden Days* (1947), p.174.

15. 'The historical evolution of property, in fact and in idea', in Charles Gore (introduction), *Property, its rights and duties* (1913) p.27. My italics.

16. *Social Evolution and Political Theory* (New York, 1911), p.182.

17. *The Metaphysical Theory of the State* (1918), p.24.

18. Introduction to second edition, p.xxxvi.

19. Ibid., p.xxxviii. On this point cf. Melvin Richter, *The Politics of Conscience. T.H. Green and his age* (1964), pp.132-4.

20. Professor James Sully, *Speaker*, 10 Dec. 1904, p.265.

21. Hobhouse to Scott, 6 June 1901.

22. Note to 'The philosophy of development' (1924) reprinted in L.T. Hobhouse, *Sociology and Philosophy. A centenary collection of essays and articles* (1966), p.296.

23. See D.G. Ritchie, *The Principles of State Interference* (1891), pp.143-5.

24. *Memoir*, p.32.

25. *The Roots of Modern Sociology* (University of London, 1908), p.10.

26. *Memoir*, p.79.

27. *The Man* versus *the State* (1884), edited by Donald MacRae (Pelican classics, 1969), p.67.

28. *Social Evolution and Political Theory*, pp.86, 204.

29. Cp. T.H. Green, *Lectures on the Principles of Political Obligation* (1895), paras. 20-21. This seems the more conclusive since Hobhouse quotes from them approvingly in *The Metaphysical Theory of the State*, pp.118-19; and in his discussion of this question in *The Labour Movement*, pp.89-90, he uses para. 31 in support.

30. P.90.

31. The preface to *Mind in Evolution* contains an acknowledgement to Ward, *q.v.* Richard Hofstadter, *Social Darwinism in American Thought* (Philadelphia, 1945), ch.4.

32. *The Roots of Modern Sociology*, p.17.

33. *The Decline of Liberalism* (L.T. Hobhouse Memorial Trust Lecture, No. 10; Oxford, 1940), pp.12-13.

34. *Social Evolution and Political Theory*, p.160.

35. *Evolution and Society. A study in Victorian social theory* (1966; 2nd edn. 1970), p.273.

36. See *Social Evolution and Political Theory*, p.157.

37. *The Metaphysical Theory of the State*, p.15.

38. *Social Evolution and Political Theory*, p.158; cf. p.161 where he takes a more positive view.

39. *Great Contemporaries* (1937; Fontana edn. 1959), p.81.

40. P. 259.

41. 'The philosophy of development', *Sociology and Philosophy*, p.330.

42. P.79.

43. *Property, its rights and duties*, p.21.

44. Pp.51, 97.

45. *Manchester Guardian*, 7 July 1899.

46. *Government by the People* (London, People's Suffrage Federation, 1910), p.24.

47. *In the Golden Days*, p.174.

48. Introduction to second edition, p.xv.

49. *Viz*. Shaw. See Textual note 38.

50. *Memoir*, p.30.

51. *The Labour Movement*, p.4.

52. Scott to Hobhouse, 3 June 1899.

53. Leader, *Manchester Guardian*, 7 July 1899.

54. Hobhouse to Scott, 7 Nov. 1924, in Trevor Wilson (ed.), *The Political Diaries of C.P. Scott, 1911-1928* (1970), p.468; cf. introduction to second edition, p.xxxiii.

55. Second edition, p.xxxi.

56. Ibid., p.213 n.

57. *C.P. Scott, 1846-1932. The making of the 'Manchester Guardian'*, p.41.

58. Second edition, pp.xx-xxi.

59. *Memoir*, p.74.

DEMOCRACY AND REACTION

IMPORTANT NEW WORKS.

Bygones Worth Remembering.
A Sequel to Sixty Years of an Agitator's Life.
> By GEORGE JACOB HOLYOAKE. 2 vols. Demy 8vo. 21s.

The Hungry Forties.
Life Under the Bread Tax.
> Letters and other Testimonies of Contemporary Witnesses. With Introduction by Mrs. COBDEN UNWIN. Large crown 8vo. Cloth, 6s.

The Life of Richard Cobden.
> By the Right Hon. JOHN MORLEY, M.P. Popular Edition, cloth, 2s. 6d. net. Abridged Edition, paper covers, 6d. Library Edition, 2 vols., 3s. 6d. each.

My Memory of Gladstone.
> By GOLDWIN SMITH. With Portrait. Crown 8vo, cloth, 2s. 6d. net.

The Opportunity of Liberalism.
> By BROUGHAM VILLIERS. Paper boards, 1s. net.

The English People.
A Study of their Political Psychology.
> By ÉMILE BOUTMY. With an Introduction by J. E. C. BODLEY. Cloth, 16s.

The Society of To=Morrow.
A Forecast of Its Political Organisation.
> By G. DE MOLINARI. With an Introduction by HODGSON PRATT. Cloth, 6s.

Democracy and Reaction.
> By L. T. HOBHOUSE, Author of "The Labour Movement," "Mind in Evolution," &c. Large crown 8vo. Cloth, 5s. net.

T. FISHER UNWIN, PUBLISHER, LONDON, E.C.

DEMOCRACY AND
REACTION

BY

L. T. HOBHOUSE

AUTHOR OF "THE LABOUR MOVEMENT," "MIND IN
EVOLUTION," ETC.

LONDON: T. FISHER UNWIN
PATERNOSTER SQUARE. 1904

NOTE

SOME of the questions with which this volume is concerned were dealt with by the writer in a series of articles published in the *Speaker* between two and three years ago. Parts of these articles are incorporated in the present work, principally in Chapters VI. and VII.

The writer has to thank Lord Hobhouse and Mr. and Mrs. J. L. Hammond for many valuable suggestions and criticisms.

CONTENTS

CHAPTER I

DURING some twenty, or it may be thirty years, a wave of reaction has spread over the civilised world and invaded one department after another of thought and action. This is no unprecedented occurrence. In the onward movement of mankind history shows us each forward step followed by a pause, and too often by a backsliding in which much of the ground gained is lost. Of the causes of this almost rhythmical, yet tragic, alternation we know little. Sometimes it would seem that the forces gathered together to remove some obstruction which directly blocks advance become themselves a hindrance to further movement. Sometimes the ideas which fill one generation with enthusiasm appear as though spent and worn when the next age arrives, while their work is but half done. They have not even the strength to inspire resistance to its undoing. Though true as ever, they have lost their moving force, and before it can advance again the world must wait for some fresh word of the prophet to make all things new. Meanwhile the mind of the people is empty, swept, and garnished ready for the entrance of bad teaching and spurious philosophy. To which of these causes is the reaction of our time to be mainly attributed? Is it that the Democratic State, the special creation of the modern world, and the pivot of the humanitarian movement, has itself become an obstruction to progress? Does popular government, with the influence which it gives to the Press and the platform, necessarily entail a blunting of moral sensibility, a cheapening and vulgarisation of national ideals, an extended scope for canting rhetoric and poor sophistry as a cover for the realities of the brutal rule of wealth? Are these evils of popular government essential and inevitable, and if so, does it mean that the work of generations of reformers must be undone?

Or should we rather trace the reaction to the temper of the time and the mode of thought prevailing in the world ? Is it that after the great reforming movement of the nineteenth century a period of lassitude has set in ; that the ideals of the reform era have lost their efficacy, that its watchwords cease to move, while the blank thus left is filled in by shallow philosophies or sheer materialism ?

The question is the more interesting at the present time, because of late the ideas of the reform period have shown signs of revival. The reaction has gone deep enough to touch, as it were, a quick, and has stung the social conscience into activity.

It may be that this activity is the beginning of a new life. Indeed, it is not impossible that the year 1903 will be regarded by historians as marking the end, and therefore also the beginning of an era in political thought. The sudden attack upon Free Trade in the middle of the year was hardly more unexpected than the solid strength of the defence offered by the established fiscal system. It might well have been thought beforehand that Free Trade was destined to

go the way of other political reforms which
belonged to the same epoch and rested at
bottom on the same principles. It had long
been recognised that the Liberalism of
Cobden's day was in a state of disintegration.
The old cry of peace, retrenchment and
reform had for many years ceased to awaken
any response. The ideal of peace had given
way to that of extended dominion. Retrenchment was impossible as long as new
territories were constantly being acquired
and retained by force, and the demand for
domestic reform was silenced by the impera-
tive clamour of foreign difficulties or frontier
entanglements. The conceptions of personal
freedom, of national rights, of international
peace, had been relegated by practical men to
the lumber-room of disused ideas. The whole
set of conceptions which group themselves
about the idea of liberty appeared to be outworn and unsuited to the needs of a generation bent on material progress and impatient
of moral restraint. But now in relation to
the fiscal question the discarded ideals have
shown an unexpected vitality while the drift
of the newer teaching has also become clearer.

The reaction has received a check. New forces have arisen and energies that slumbered and slept have been awakened. It would seem as though after all Free Trade would stand against the tide that has swept away so many landmarks of political reform and moral progress.

Cobden himself would have held it strange that Free Trade should remain the only abiding monument of his work. We may almost say he would have thought it impossible—for Free Trade to him was no isolated doctrine but part of a very compact political system. Cobden saw politics as a whole in which the parts were very closely united. Free Trade, non-interference, a policy of peace, the reduction of armaments, retrenchment of expenditure, popular government at home, self-government for the Colonies—these were not, as he conceived them, isolated views any one of which might be taken up or discarded without affecting the remainder. They were strictly interdependent. They were connected in principle and in practical working. A single passage will serve to illustrate this point.

Cobden is speaking of what he has done for agriculture, but the passage is given here not for that reason, but as a terse and clear statement of the main points of his creed and their mutual connections. Insisting that it had been his constant aim to reduce the burdens falling upon agriculture by way of compensation for the temporary difficulties which he saw would result from the adoption of Free Trade, Cobden says—

" It was with that view that I preferred my budget, and advocated the reduction of our armaments; it is with that view, coupled with higher motives, that I have recommended arbitration treaties, to render unnecessary the vast amount of armaments which are kept up between civilised countries. It is with that view—the view of largely reducing the expenditure of the State, and giving relief, especially for the agricultural classes—that I have made myself the object of the sarcasms of those very parties, by going to Paris to attend peace meetings. It is with that view that I have directed attention to our Colonies, showing how you might be carrying out the principle of Free Trade, give to the Colonies self-government, and charge them, at the same time, with the expense of their own government." *

Peace, arbitration, Colonial self-government, reduction of armaments, retrenchment, Free

* Speech at Leeds, printed in " The Manchester School," by F. W. Hirst, p. 251.

Trade, all are here. The link between them in this passage, it will be seen, is expenditure. This was the practical connection. War meant expenditure. The old system of holding the Colonies by force meant expenditure, and expenditure involved indirect taxation and made Free Trade virtually impossible. Conversely, Free Trade would diminish the commercial inducements to military aggression, and by limiting taxation to forms in which any increment is immediately felt as a palpable burden, would incline men to look at both sides of the question before plunging into war. Cobden is often mocked as a false prophet, sometimes very unjustly. But the function of a true political thinker is not to predict events, but to point out causal connections. The adoption of Free Trade by this country has not brought universal peace, but events have certainly justified Cobden's view that Protectionism is a heavy makeweight on the side of militarism and war. Again, few considering fairly the temper of our own time would deny that expenditure is the main restraining force which keeps a nation that has secured itself against attack from undue interference with its neighbours. In days of prosperity Jeshurun waxes fat, the war passions are readily excited, the appeal to justice or humanity is heard with impatience and stifled by counter-appeals to the civilising mission of a great nation. It is only when the bill comes in, and is perchance longer than was anticipated, that people become ready once again to listen to reason. Thus in the practical working out expenditure was the meeting-point of Cobden's principles. There was, of course, a deeper connection—a connection of idea. The same principle of liberty runs through it all. Trade was to be free from the trammels of State interference; the Colonies were to be free from the domination of the Mother Country; foreign nations were to be free from intervention, and were to work out for themselves their own salvation. The unimpeded development of human faculty was the mainspring of progress, so that freedom for the individual and for the community—freedom in religion, in politics, in industry, and in trade—must be the watchword of the reformer.

Such a theory of government, so many-sided and yet so simple, challenges criticism from many points of view, and in the event it has been the fate of Cobdenism to be attacked from the two most opposite sides, both by those who wanted to go further and by those who wanted to go back. To some reformers Cobden's creed appeared negative and cold. This was in part a misconception. The Cobdenite, like the Benthamite, was a believer in human progress and held its furtherance to be the supreme end and aim of the politician.

"I have gone into politics," said W. J. Fox, "with this question constantly in my mind—What will your theories, your forms, your propositions, do for human nature? Will they make man more manly? Will they raise men and women in the scale of creation? Will they lift them above the brutes? Will they call forth their thoughts, their feelings, their actions? Will they make them moral beings? Will they be worthy to tread the earth as children of the common Parent, and to look forward, not only for His blessing here, but for His benignant bestowment of happiness hereafter? If institutions do this, I applaud them; if they have lower aims, I despise them; and if they have antagonistic aims, I counteract them with all my might and strength." *

* Speech at Oldham, in "The Manchester School," p. 491.

This confession of faith by a typical Cobdenite is positive enough in ultimate principle. The negative side appears in the conception of the means by which progress is to be achieved, since improvement was expected rather from the removal of barriers which cramp individual enterprise than from the positive intervention of the State on behalf of social reform. But even here there are qualifications of the Cobdenite doctrine which are too often forgotten. Not only was Cobden for Free Education—a generation ahead of his time—but he was no less emphatically for restricting the labour of children. "No child," he wrote to Hunt, "ought to be put to work in a cotton mill at all so early as the age of thirteen years," being in this fully two generations ahead of his time. These things are too often forgotten when Cobden is criticised as an opponent of the factory acts.

But when all allowances are made it must be admitted that later thinkers found Cobden's theory of the functions of the State in industrial matters to be negative and unsatisfying. How far there is a real cleavage of principle

between the old and newer Liberalism will
be discussed at a later stage. Here we have
only to remark that though the breach of
continuity may be less deep than appears at
first, it was felt as a real breach. Comparatively few observers * realised the underlying principle, the vivid conception of what
is actually required by the common good
as against the dominant interest, which
connected the old and new in spirit and
intention. The majority were content to
insist that the Manchester School was dead,
while many displayed towards it an ani-
mosity from which the dead are generally
exempt. This was but one of the inevitable

* T. H. Green is a notable exception. " The passion
for improving mankind, in its ultimate object, does not
vary. But the immediate object of reformers and the
forms of persuasion by which they seek to advance
them, vary much in different generations. To a hasty
observer they might even seem contradictory, and to
justify the notion that nothing better than a desire for
change, selfish or perverse, is at the bottom of all
reforming movements. Only those who will think a
little longer about it can discern the same old cause of
social good against class interests, for which, under
altered names, Liberals are fighting now as they were
fifty years ago." (Works, vol. iii. p. 367.)

misunderstandings of political development, but the unfortunate part of it was that it undermined the old Liberalism from the side of domestic politics and in the minds of progressive thinkers just as a serious attack was impending on it from the side of Imperial politics and in the interests of reaction. The socialistic development of Liberalism paved the way for Imperialism by diminishing the credit of the school which had stood most stoutly for the doctrines of liberty, fair dealing, and forbearance in international affairs. So non-intervention abroad went by the board along with *laissez faire* at home ; national liberty was ranked with competitive industrialism as an exploded superstition ; a positive theory of the State in domestic affairs was matched by a positive theory of Empire, and the way was made straight for Imperialism, the meaning and rise of which must now be briefly studied for themselves.

CHAPTER II

THE IMPERIAL IDEA

PARADOXICAL as it may seem, the new conception of Empire had its roots, politically speaking, in the older Liberalism. For it was the older Liberalism which made the Colonial Empire what it was, and it was to that Empire as Liberalism had made it that Imperialist sentiment in the first instance appealed. The appeal was, in this form, very difficult to resist. " See," the Imperialist would say, " this marvellous work of our race, this vast inheritance of the generations which we hold in trust for our descendants—in mere size the greatest empire of history, in variety of interest, in the extraordinary complexity of its composition far surpassing all political societies which the world has ever known. Consider how it extends the law of peace over prairie and jungle, mountain and steppe, subarctic ice and torrid forest; how it maintains order and administers justice with equal success for the brand-new mining community, for the ancient civilisation of the Ganges or the Nile, or for the primitive clan of the Indian hills. Is not this," urges the enthusiast, " among the greatest of human achievements, this unparalleled adaptability in the arts of conquest and of government? And yet this is not the best. What is an infinitely greater matter is that where the British flag goes, go British freedom, British justice, an absolutely incorruptible civil service, a scrupulous impartiality as between religion and races, an enthusiasm for the spread of that individual liberty and local self-government which have made England herself so great! Are you insensible to these achievements of your country, and can you not rise above the narrow patriotism —by comparison a 'parochial' view—which is limited to one small island. You talk perhaps of humanity—a vague, abstract idea. But do you not see that any genuine humanitarianism must be the result of a gradual

broadening of those very sympathies which
first make a man a good patriot ? There was
a time when love for England, as a whole,
was too wide a conception, and men were
Mercians or Northumbrians, but not Englishmen. Just as it was an advance when the
love for England superseded this narrow
provincialism, so is it an advance when
Imperialism supersedes your narrow Little
Englandism, and if there is ever to be any
genuine cosmopolitanism, any world State
commanding a world's devotion, it must be
reached by this road and none other. You
dream, it may be, of universal peace. How
is universal peace to come save through the
establishment of a common authority to hold
the petty nations in awe, and where else will
you find the people capable of wielding such
authority with due regard for local freedom
and national differences except in your own
country? You may say that Empire means
force, aggression, conquest. That may have
been so in the past, but we live in an age
when Empire is free, tolerant and unaggressive, and if we still acquire territory
we acquire it not for ourselves but for civilisa-

tion.* You may object to the methods by which the Empire was built up, but here it is in being—a great fact, a tremendous responsibility. You could not be quit of it if you wished. Take it up then as the most sacred trust, and do not let it go in craven fear of being great."

The appeal was seductive, and taken at its face value, that is to say, without analysis of the political facts on which it was based, almost irresistible. One caveat indeed might be entered. The use of the term "Little Englander" as a term of scorn does not consist well with a "patriotic" or even an accurate view of our history. It might

* ". . . We, in our Colonial policy, as fast as we acquire new territory and develop it, develop it as trustees of civilisation for the commerce of the world. We offer in all these markets over which our flag floats the same opportunities, the same open field, to foreigners that we offer to our own subjects, and upon the same terms. In that policy we stand alone, because all other nations, as fast as they acquire new territory—acting, as I believe, most mistakenly in their own interests, and, above all, in the interests of the countries that they administer—all other nations seek at once to secure the monopoly for their own products by preferential and artificial methods. . . ." (Mr. Chamberlain at the Birmingham Chamber of Commerce, November 13, 1896.)

fairly be asked in reply whether there was nothing to be proud of in " Little England," in her history, her literature, her thought, the great men that she has borne for the world, her struggle for political and religious freedom ? The question might be raised whether the British Empire as a whole has any history to show which compares with the history of "Little England"; any science, any literature, any art ; in fine, any great collective military achievement, worthy to be weighed in the scale against the resistance of " Little England " to Philip II. or to Napoleon. A great Imperialist once coupled the name of " Little England " with the policy of surrender. It was a libel. Little England never surrendered. On the contrary, she three times encountered Powers which aspired to the mastery of the world, and three times overthrew them. The genuine pride of patriotism is surely lost when littleness of geographical extent can be construed into a term of reproach. It is the other face of the same vulgarity which boasts that a single British colony is greater than the land which produced Kant and Goethe. Little

Englander is a name of which no patriot need fear to boast.

Be this as it may, it must be conceded that the Imperialist appeal was seductive, and to the modern Liberal the more so because the Empire as he knows it is the creation of earlier Liberalism. By the admission of all parties, if the Empire was good it was good because it had been reconciled with liberty, and this reconciliation had been the work of the Manchester School and the "Philosophic Radicals." Those who are taunted with a narrow and unimaginative indifference to the Colonies are precisely those who championed Colonial freedom and so built up the Colonial Empire as we have known it. It was not the Colonies but the old "Colonial system" to which men like Cobden avowed their antagonism, and that Colonial system meant a political and commercial despotism to which separation was certainly preferable.

The eighteenth-century view of a Colony was that it was necessarily dependent, politically and commercially, on the Mother Country. When the crisis of the American controversy came, Fox and Burke saw that

this theory was incompatible with the principles of English liberty, and that if it
prevailed it must be fatal not only to the
Americans, but ultimately to the constitutional liberties of Englishmen. They recognised, in short, that the Imperialism of their
day was no more compatible in the long run
with liberty at home than abroad. But if
Colonies could not be governed by the
Mother Country for her own good, it might
be argued, and by some it was argued, that
they were merely a burden. In fact, from
the time of the American War onwards
there were these two considerations tending
to shape Liberal opinion in relation to the
Empire. The main consideration was that,
as a matter of principle, distant dependencies
inhabited by white men admittedly capable
of self-government ought not to be subjected
to the rule of a Colonial Secretary who had
perhaps never been within two thousand
miles of their borders. The other consideration was that if England was debarred by
justice from making use of them for her own
ends, they could not claim in justice that she
should protect them.

But the Radicals did not desire separation for its own sake. Their leading principle was Colonial self-government. They were told by opponents that this meant separation, and those who believed this accepted separation as an inevitable consequence. In other words, they put self-government first and the Imperial connection second.

But events showed that this was the very way by which the Imperial connection was to be preserved. This is fully grasped in the Durham Report on Canada—the classical exposition of the application of Radical or Benthamist ideas to the Colonial Empire. Here the gift of responsible government is explicitly urged as the only method of retaining Canada as a permanent member of the Empire :—

" I do not anticipate that a Colonial Legislature, thus strong and thus self-governing, would desire to abandon the connection with Great Britain. On the contrary, I believe that the practical relief from undue interference, which would be the result of such a change, would strengthen the present bond of feelings and interests ; and that the connection would only become more durable and advantageous, by having more of equality, of freedom, and of local independence. But at any rate, our first duty is to secure the well-being of our Colonial country-men ; and if in the hidden decrees of that wisdom by which this world is ruled, it is written that these countries are not for ever to remain portions of the Empire, we owe it to our honour to take good care, that, when they separate from us, they should not be the only countries on the American continent in which the Anglo-Saxon race shall be found unfit to govern itself.

"I am, in truth, so far from believing that the increased power and weight that would be given to these Colonies by union would endanger their connection with the Empire, that I look to it as the only means of fostering such a national feeling throughout them as would effectually counterbalance whatever tendencies may now exist towards separation. No large community of free and intelligent men will long feel contented with a political system which places them, because it places their country, in a position of inferiority to their neighbours." *

The attitude of the Radicals was clearly expressed by Molesworth in 1848 :—

"I do not propose to abandon the American Colonies; but if we are compelled to choose between the alternative of the continuation of the present vast expenditure and that of abandoning these Colonies, it is evident that the latter alternative would be the more profitable one in an economical point of view. But I maintain that if we govern our North American Colonies as we ought to govern them, follow out vigorously the principle of responsible government and leave them to manage their own affairs uncontrolled by the Colonial Office, we may with safety diminish our military force and expenditure,

* A Report on Canada, p. 229. (Methuen.)

and they will willingly continue to be our fellow
subjects." *

And again :—

"For what purpose do we keep 9,000 troops in
America? Is it to protect the colonists against the
United States? But if they are loyal at heart they are
strong enough to protect themselves; if they are disloyal,
twice 9,000 men will not keep them down." †

To the same effect Cobden :—

"People tell me I want to abandon our Colonies; but
I say, do you intend to hold your Colonies by the sword,
by armies, and ships of war? That is not a permanent
hold upon them. I want to retain them by their affec-
tions." ‡

The essence of the Radical view then was
that Imperial Union rests on the free consent
of the Colonies.§   As a general principle, this

* Speech in the House of Commons, 1848. "Manchester School," p. 419.

† Ibid., p. 418.

‡ "Speeches," p. 249. On some occasions, however
Cobden leant more decidedly to separation as the simplest
solution. See Morley's "Life," vol. ii. p. 471.

§ This view was already shared by Mr. Gladstone in the
later forties, though he repudiated Molesworth's deduction from it that we ought to wish success to the
Canadians even when in arms against the Home Government :—

". . . Experience has proved that if you want to

view has gained complete acceptance, and is now among the commonplaces of Imperialism.*

strengthen the connection between the Colonies and this country—if you want to see British law held in respect and British institutions adopted and beloved in the Colonies, never associate with them the hated name of force and coercion exercised by us, at a distance, over their rising fortunes. Govern them upon a principle of freedom. Defend them against aggression from without. Regulate their foreign relations. These things belong to the Colonial connection. But of the duration of that connection let them be the judges, and I predict that if you leave them the freedom of judgment, it is hard to say when the day will come when they will wish to separate from the great name of England. Depend upon it, they covet a share in that great name. You will find in that feeling of theirs the greatest security for the connection. . . . You have seen various Colonies, some of them lying at the antipodes, offering to you their contributions to assist in supporting the wives and families of your soldiers, the heroes that have fallen in the war. This, I venture to say, may be said without exaggeration to be among the firstfruits of that system upon which, within the last twelve or fifteen years, you have founded a rational mode of administering the affairs of your Colonies without gratuitous interference." (Morley's "Gladstone," vol. i. p. 363.)

* "We talk of our Colonies. You know they are not ours in any sense whatever of possession. They are absolutely independent States. There is nothing to prevent their separating from us to-morrow. We could

By the gradual extension of self-government the anticipations of Lord Durham and Sir W. Molesworth were amply realised, and by the last decade of the century it appeared that the problem of reconciling Empire with liberty had been solved. The Imperial factor in the Colonies was represented by plain men of the rough-and-ready British type. Perhaps they were not always up-to-date. They were not skilled in identifying patriotism with their own party. Few of them understood the art of working the press, and none could for long have maintained a reputation for omniscience on a record of repeated errors. Their dispatches were prosaically accurate, and in the columns of a sensational newspaper would have appeared dull. They were not invariably prophesying, and when they did prophesy they were not invariably wrong. They were not specially skilled in finding precedents for in-

not, we would not, attempt to hold them by force. It is a voluntary bond, and a bond the obligations of which have never up to the present time been defined." (Mr. Chamberlain at Rochester, July 26, 1904.)

This principle is not the less valuable because it states succinctly and in general terms the political case against the speaker's South African policy.

justice. They made no royal progresses and few epoch-making speeches. Altogether they were dull fellows, it is to be feared. Certainly they were not more than Englishmen, and did not aspire to be. Yet somehow they built up a reputation for holding the balance of government fairly, and telling the home public the truth. They kept clear of the financial interests. They acted as representatives of the Crown, and yet made little fuss about their personal position.

Under this mild sway each component State of the Empire enjoyed full internal self-government, and yet the whole had advantages which small free States cannot claim. Over a great area of the world there was, it seemed, assured peace ; there was the machinery for adjusting disputes between different parts, should such disputes arise ; and there was the consciousness of a wider fraternity, of a vaster common heritage, than the citizens of any small community, however proud, could enjoy. In all this, taken in full sincerity, there was much to appeal to Liberals, little to repel them.

A critic might indeed point out that the

Colonies are not the whole Empire. There are the tropical dependencies, with some seven-eighths of the Empire's population, and no pretence of self-government. We rule them only by frankly throwing over all democratic principles and admitting that they are not applicable except to white men. "True or false," the critic might proceed, "this admission has certainly weakened the fibre of English democratic sentiment. After all, the white man's claim to rule the black because he is wiser and more capable is essentially the same as the noble's claim to rule the commonalty for their good as much as for his own. The claim may be justified by the facts in the one case and not justified in the other, but the mode of reasoning is so similar that it is very hard to admit the one and refuse the other. Here, then," he might urge, "Imperialist and democratic sentiments must come into conflict." But to this criticism there was a double answer, which on the whole allayed any uneasiness that might have arisen. The first was that from the practical point of view there was no real option in the matter. Granted that it might conceivably have been better for both countries that India had never been conquered, there was the Indian Empire in being, a realised fact which nothing could get over, a responsibility that could no more be shaken off than the responsibility for Cornwall. The first duty of statesmen was not with general principles but with the way to make the best of the actual situation; and— here the second consideration came in—on the whole a good best was being made of India. We gave her, if not self-government, at least good government. We governed largely by Indian ideas, interfering with them only when, as in the case of Suttee, they too palpably outraged European sentiment. As to self-government, we at least respected the village community and made honest attempts at local autonomy on a larger scale.

Such then was the creed of Empire as drawn up in particular for the man of Liberal sympathies. He was to enter with enthusiasm into the heritage won by the energy of his fathers and ennobled by the great principles of an earlier generation of Liberals. In this heritage, whatever was of doubtful morality belonged to the past. As it now stood the Empire was a guarantee of peace, freedom and equality between races and religions, and a force making for righteousness and civilisation throughout the world, while Imperialism meant nothing but loyalty and devotion to an Empire so constituted.

But was this what Imperialism meant? A political theory must be judged not only by its profession but by its fruits. What, then, were the fruits of Imperialism, i.e., of the actual policy urged by Imperialists and defended on the ground of Imperial necessity? Did it, for example, give us peace? On the contrary, the perplexed observer, looking vainly for the British peace which was to be, was confronted with an endless succession of frontier wars, some small, some great, but all ending with the annexation of further territory. Under the reign of Imperialism the temple of Janus is never closed. Blood never ceases to run. The voice of the mourner is never hushed. Of course, in every case some excellent reason has been forthcoming. We were invariably on the defensive. We had no intention of going to war. Having gone to war, we had no intention of occupying the country. Having occupied the country provisionally, we were still determined not to annex it. Having annexed it, we were convinced that the whole process was inevitable from first to last. On each several occasion we acted purely on the defensive, and on each several occasion we ended by occupying the land of our aggressive neighbours. Such is the fiction still solemnly maintained. The naked fact is that we are maintaining a distinct policy of aggressive warfare on a large scale and with great persistence, and the only result of attempting constantly to blink the fact is to have introduced an atmosphere of self-sophistication, or in one syllable, of cant into our politics which is perhaps more corrupting than the unblushing denial of right. No less than one third of the present territory of the Empire and one quarter of its population have been acquired since 1870, and the bulk of the increase dates from 1884, *i.e.*, it falls within the period during which Imperialism has become a conscious influence. And notwithstanding the disappointments attending on the

South African adventure there is as yet no sign of slackening.*

Meanwhile, partly through the direct needs of the conquered territories, partly through the dangerous jealousies awakened by the march of Empire, but most of all through the mood of nervous suspicion engendered among ourselves by the consciousness of our aggressions, the policy of expansion fastens on us an ever-increasing burden of military and naval expenditure. The following table shows the total expenditure in both branches

* Mr. Hobson ("Imperialism," p. 20) gives the following list of territories acquired between 1884 and 1900 (inclusive) :—

British New Guiana	Rhodesia
Nigeria	Zanzibar
Pondoland	British Central Africa
Somaliland	Uganda
Bechuanaland	Ashantee
Upper Burma	Wei-hai-Wei
British East Africa	Kow-lung
Zululand (with Tongaland)	Soudan
Sarawak	Transvaal and Orange River
Pahang (Straits Settlements)	Colony.

The total area of these territories amounts to 3,711,957 square miles, and the population is estimated at about 57,000,000.

of the service in 1870, before the revival of Imperialism began; in 1895, when the Unionist Government returned to power; in 1898–9, the year before the South African War; and in the present year. The total expenditure of each year is also given.

	Naval and Military expenditure. 000's omitted.	Total expenditure. 000's omitted.
1875	24,507	73,605
1895	35,595	93,918
1899	44,283	108,150
1904	72,153	146,961

The meaning of this table may be put in one sentence. Militarism, based on Imperialism, has eaten up the national resources which should have gone to improve the condition of the people.*

Thus the peace promised by Imperialism

* In the early part of 1899 the movement in favour of a scheme of old-age pensions was at its height. The barrier was want of funds. The cost of any scheme of "universal" pensions was put at some twenty millions, and it appeared hopeless to ask the public to consent to so vast an increase in expenditure for such an object as the happiness of the aged poor and the thorough-going reform of the poor law. Yet within the few years that have passed, nearly twice the number of millions required have been added—for the benefit of whom?

has not been realised. Freedom has fared no better. Of all the acquisitions above mentioned, not a single one has, as yet, become self-governing. In the case of the Orange Free State, one of the most liberally governed, best administered, and prosperous communities of the world has been converted into a land of desolation,* subjected for the past two years to a despotism as absolute as that of Russia. No Irish Coercion Act has ever approached the arbitrary powers taken by Government under the Peace Preservation Ordinance, applying to the Orange Colony and the Transvaal, by which men can be arrested and imprisoned for twenty-one days without being charged with any offence, † by which they can be

---

* Or, in Lord Milner's words, a country "absolutely denuded of everything." (Bluebook, Cd. 155.) It was undoubtedly the desire of the British public that the devastation should be repaired; but, unfortunately, apart from any question of its administration, the grant made for the purpose was hopelessly out of proportion to the amount of the damage.

† Clauses 10 and 11 of the Ordinance run as follows :—

10. It shall be lawful for any Magistrate, Assistant

expelled from home, lands, and country on fourteen days' notice without trial and without cause shown, by the mere fiat of the Lieutenant-Governor, * by which, finally, any act or word supposed to bring Lord Milner

Magistrate, or Police Officer in any district to arrest or cause to be arrested without warrant any person in such district on reasonable suspicion of his having committed treason or any of the offences mentioned in section 18 of this Ordinance and to lodge such person in any gaol in the said district.

11. Upon the written order of such Magistrate, Assistant Magistrate, or Police Officer as aforesaid, the gaoler of the said district shall be bound to receive and detain in custody in the gaol thereof any such person arrested as aforesaid for such time as is specified in the said order, or if no time is specified therein, until the said gaoler receives an order from the Attorney-General or official on whose order the said person is detained for such person's release, notwithstanding that no charge is preferred against such person either at the time of his arrest or of his reception into gaol; provided that every such person shall be entitled to his discharge from gaol or custody unless within twenty-one days after such imprisonment criminal proceedings shall be commenced against him.

* Clause 24. It shall be lawful for the Lieutenant-Governor on its being shown to his satisfaction that there are reasonable grounds for believing that any person within this Colony is dangerous to the peace

into hatred and contempt * may be punished by five years' penal servitude. Such is the

and good government of the country to issue order under the hand of the Colonial Secretary to such person to leave the Colony within fourteen days after service of such order.

* A seditious intention is an intention :

(1) To bring His Majesty or the Governor or Lieutenant-Governor of the Transvaal in person into hatred or contempt; or

(2) To excite disaffection against His Majesty or the Governor or Lieutenant-Governor in person or the Government and Constitution of the United Kingdom or of the Transvaal as by law established or the administration of justice therein ; or

(3) To incite His Majesty's subjects to attempt to procure otherwise than by lawful means the alteration of any matter in the Transvaal by law established ; or

(4) To incite any person to commit any crime in disturbance of the public peace ; or

(5) To raise discontent and disaffection amongst His Majesty's subjects ; or

(6) To promote feelings of ill-will and hostility between different classes of His Majesty's subjects ;

Provided that no one shall be deemed to have a seditious intention only because he intends in good faith—

(a) To show that His Majesty or the Governor or Lieutenant-Governor has been misled or mistaken in his measures ; or

(b) To point out errors or defects in the Government or Constitution of the United Kingdom or the Transvaal

result of the campaign for "equal rights for all white men south of the Zambesi." Such was the promise of Imperialism, and such is its performance. And it is by contrasts of this kind that the general opinion of its merits is gradually being modified.

It may be said that these deviations from a general principle are mere temporary expedients imposed by the necessities of a perilous situation. Unfortunately, they easily become precedents. * Nor can we leave out of sight that in South Africa this temporary despotism, while vaguely promising some form of constitutional government in the near future, has first arranged for the

as by law established or in the administration of justice therein with a view to the reformation of such alleged errors or defects; or to urge His Majesty's subjects to attempt to procure by lawful means the alteration of any matter in the Transvaal by law established.

* Already it has been suggested by the Attorney-General of the Transvaal to apply the arbitrary powers of expulsion under the Peace Preservation Act as a means of getting rid of children of Chinese born in the country. A power designed for a temporary political exigency may readily be converted into a permanent expedient of arbitrary government to serve quite another purpose.

practical maintenance of close oligarchical rule, by replacing white by yellow labour, the admitted motive being the fear of the political power of the white workman.*

But, to quit this extreme case, we cannot find elsewhere that freedom and equality have been fostered by territorial extension. On the contrary, that spirit of domination which rejoices in conquest is by nature hostile to the idea of racial equality, and indifferent to political liberty. The experiments in the direction of self-government in India have not been developed. The tendency is rather to curtail the measure of freedom already granted, and to restrict the opportunities opened to natives of India in the last generation, of taking part in the government of the country. The literature of Imperialism is openly contemptuous—sometimes aggressively, sometimes patronisingly—of the "coloured" races, and scoffs at the old Liberal conception of opening to them the road to self-development, and alternates between a sentimental insistence on the duties owed to them by the white man,

* Cf. p. 43 note.

and invective against any one who inquires
how those duties are being performed. Nor
is it only political freedom that has suffered.
There are ominous indications of a recrudescence of servile labour. It is not, indeed,
possible for a fully developed system of
slave-holding to revive all at once. But
there are numberless gradations between
absolute chattel slavery, and the complete
personal freedom of the modern white
workman. In many popular discussions of
the question it seems to be assumed that
the term slavery is only applicable where
one human being is as much the property of
another as his ox or his ass. But this
view is not sustained by the facts, since in
most civilised, and in some barbaric countries,
which admit the institution, the slave is, in
varying degrees, protected from ill-usage,
and, in some cases, he cannot be sold or
disposed of without his own consent. Another
common assumption is that a labour contract
cannot be of a servile character if the labourer
enters upon it freely, and with his eyes open.
This also is erroneous. It is a feature of
many slave systems, ancient and modern, that

a man who has no other means of livelihood, or perhaps of satisfying his creditors, may assign himself as a slave. But if he does so, he is not the less a slave because his original act was voluntary. If self-enslavement were tolerated, we might easily be confronted with the revival of a slave class in our own country, which would be augmented in every recurring period of distress. The truth is that there is no single and sufficient mark by which to determine the precise degree of unfreedom which deserves the name of slavery. The points of unfreedom or servility are many, and where there is either compulsion to work (as in the case of the Matabele and the Bechuana), or grave restraints on personal liberty which are not necessary for the performance of the labour contract, as in the case of the Chinese on the Rand, we cannot but admit that the arrangement is of a servile character. Under contemporary conditions there is an ominous tendency * to resort to such systems, and what is of even worse augury, is that they

---

* The prompt suppression of the Kanaka traffic by the Commonwealth Parliament shows a counter-movement of

are justified by British Ministers and officials
with loose talk—at one time of the "dignity
of labour," which the coloured man must

the happiest augury for the future of Australia. But in
some quarters it would almost seem to be assumed that
the Colonial capitalist may as of right demand facilities
for the supply of cheap coloured labour in the lump
from the Government, and one reads discussions as to
the fair distribution and apportionment of such labour,
precisely as though the men were chattels.

After the war, the mine-owners of the Rand first of
all secured the re-imposition of the poll tax on natives.
The object of this taxation, as avowed by their witnesses
before the Boer Commission in 1897, was to compel the
native to come into the mines, and neither Sir Godfrey
Lagden nor Lord Milner could see "that it is any
' particular hardship' that the black population should
find themselves compelled to work by the necessity
of earning enough to pay their taxes." The Kaffirs
were accused of laziness because they did not choose
to come to mines, where, as we now at length
learn from the Cape Government's report (published
in Cd. 2025) they were freely flogged, frequently disappointed of the pay promised them, and subjected to
conditions which produced a death-rate of 71 per 1,000
(as against a rate of 6·4 per 1,000 for English miners).
It would be too much to say that the Kaffirs of the Rand
are slaves, but no one reading the whole report could
maintain that their condition is that of free workmen.

But the mine-owners were not satisfied with the
supply of Kaffir labour, and their next proposal was
to import hands from Uganda. It was in vain that

be taught; at another of the indignity of
working with the coloured man, which the

the manifest objections were pointed out—the difficulty
of making natives understand the terms offered them,
and the probability, amounting almost to certainty, of
a high mortality, as the result of such a transplantation.
All objections were overruled, 818 natives were imported
between June and September, of whom 67 had died
before the end of the year, and 22 in the first four
months of the present year— besides 18 killed in an
accident.   In excuse for this enormous death-rate "the
almost incredible carelessness of the natives themselves"
is duly urged, in accordance with the regular official
formula, and Lord Milner, in January, considered
himself justified in asking for 5,000 more. (Parliamentary Paper, Africa, Nov. 1904, Cd. 1950.)

But as black labour did not suffice, recourse was
had to Chinese. The seriousness of this step lies in
the vast extension of servile labour to which it opens
the door.   For here again it is possible to argue that
the Chinese labourer is not a slave, but it is not possible
to argue that he is free. As is pointed out above, the
fact on which stress is laid—that he gives his consent
to the contract—does not, even if we assume the
consent to be a reality, affect the servility of the
conditions to which he binds himself. A system which
includes the confinement of the labourer for three years
(with liberation only by special permit, not to extend
beyond forty-eight hours), which excludes him from all
other occupations and from every chance of bettering
himself, and ends by expelling him from the country—

white is justified in feeling; at another of
the need of some "stimulus" to labour, as
though there were any necessary or justifiable
stimulus to labour, beyond the desire to
satisfy natural wants by earning a fair wage
under healthy conditions.

Reference to South Africa has been necessary because it is the leading case of the
Imperialist method, and here the contrast
between the promise and performance extends
all along the line. Imperialism was to give
us a cheap and easy victory. It gave us
nearly three years' war. It was to sweep away
the abuses of a corrupt, incompetent and
over-expensive administration. The present
administration of the Transvaal is more costly
than the former, and more completely in the
hands of the capitalists. It was to abolish

such a system, whatever it be called, cannot be called
a system of free labour. It is one of those systems,
partaking of slavery, which, in successive Conventions, we
explicitly forbade the Boer Government to introduce:—

"The South African Republic renews the declaration
made in the Sand River Convention, and in the Convention of Pretoria, that no slavery or apprenticeship
partaking of slavery will be tolerated by the Government
of the said Republic." (Convention of London, 1884.)

such scandals of a corrupt oligarchy as the dynamite monopoly. The dynamite monopoly has changed hands, but remains. It was to extend the suffrage to all white men. But at present no white men have the suffrage in either colony.* It was to liberate the white population from the yoke under which they were groaning. But, having been liberated, they openly regret the old days. It was to inaugurate an era of unparalleled commercial prosperity. Yet it is the total stagnation of trade and the impending ruin of the country that are pleaded as necessitating the importation of Chinese. It was to protect the Kaffir from the Boer, but we find that the " boys wish to call back the days of the Republic." † It was to maintain the rights of our Indian fellow-subjects. But our Indian fellow-subjects are now occupied in setting forth " the respects in which the advent of British rule has left the Indian community in a worse position than under the Boer régime." ‡

---

* For the Transvaal alone a constitution with some sort of representative element is now promised. Whether this will amount to self-government remains to be seen.

† Chief Sipendu (and others) in Cd. 2025, p. 27.

‡ Sir M. Bhownaggree in Cd. 2239, p. 21.

All these contrasts, which no distortion of the facts has been altogether able to conceal, have had their effect on the public mind. For those who still doubted whether our South African policy was conceived in the interests of the Empire as a whole or of a group of financiers, a decisive test remained. The war had been proclaimed by the Government a miner's war.* It had been justified when all other arguments failed as a necessary means of procuring a magnificent outlet for British labour. When, therefore, it was known that the magnates who had posed as champions of civic freedom objected to white labour explicitly on the ground that it would bring trade unionism and the possibilities of a labour party † which would endanger their supremacy;

---

* "This war is in a certain sense a miner's war; that is to say, it has been undertaken in order that justice may be done to the miners of the Transvaal" (Mr. Chamberlain at Lichfield, October 8, 1900).

† See Mr. Percy Tarbutt's letter to Mr. Cresswell: "I have consulted the Consolidated Goldfields people, and one of the members of the Board of the Village Main Reef has consulted Messrs. Wernher, Beit and Co., and the feeling seems to be one of fear that if a large number of white men are employed on the Rand the

when their demand for Chinese labour was granted in the teeth not only of opinion at home, but of the Colonial sentiment which during the war had been the subject of so many high-sounding appeals ; when the permanence of that conquest on which so much blood had been lavished was thus imperilled for the benefit of a few wealthy corporations—then indeed a flash of light was thrown on the dark series of events which led from the Jameson Raid to the Peace of Vereeniging. The pretences were stripped from South African Imperialism and it was seen at last for the thing that it is.

The observer who was not content with fair professions but wished to know in all seriousness whither he was being led, found set before him two deeply-contrasted pictures of Imperialism—the Imperialism of promise and the Imperialism of performance—the one based on the constitution of the Empire as

same troubles will arise as are now prevalent in the Australian Colonies, *i.e.*, that the combination of the labouring classes will become so strong as to be able to more or less to dictate, not only on questions of wages, but also on political questions, by the power of their votes when a representative Government is established."

built up by Liberal statesmen, the other based on the policy of Empire as shaped by a generation of Imperialist statesmen. It is not surprising that if he had been won to the name of Imperialism by the first picture he should have been gradually repelled from it as the lineaments of the second picture became distinct. Little by little it became clearer that the new Imperialism stood, not for a widened and ennobled sense of national responsibility, but for a hard assertion of racial supremacy and material force. The test case of Armenia had shown that after all protests against selfish isolation and the craven fear of being great, the Imperialist would incur no risk and sacrifice no shadow of material interest in a disinterested service to humanity. On the contrary it was precisely the encumbrance of our Imperial responsibilities which we were told made it impossible for us to intervene. Standing alone, this great refusal might have seemed to be dictated by an over-anxious love of peace. But to the unprejudiced observer, judging Imperialism by its actual performance, no such interpretation could long remain open. He was compelled to recognise that in practice it meant perpetual warfare, battles which, where black or yellow men were concerned, became sheer massacres, campaigns which, where a resolute white race stood in the way, involved desolation unspeakable, the destruction of political and personal freedom, and the erection on their ruins of an un-English type of overpaid and incompetent officialdom, the cold-shouldering of the British immigrant and the recrudescence of servile labour. Finally comparing the battle-cry with the actual result of victory, he began to ask himself whether the enterprises on which his fellow-countrymen freely spent their blood were such as minister to the glory of the Empire and the good of humanity, or rather to the vanity of a self-confident satrap and the lucre of a capitalist. He saw moreover that this policy of unceasing warfare entails the continual increase of military burdens, and he could not be blind to the probability that the increased expenditure thus necessitated was likely to produce a cry for the " widening of the basis of taxation," which, combined with the spirit of antipathy to foreigners fostered by the same order of ideas, would result in a movement for Protection. Lastly, it became more and more probable that the difficulties of finding men to meet the constant drain of warfare would in the end necessitate some form of compulsory enlistment. Faced by the actual experience of its working, and forecasting the further results to which it must lead, our observer began to ask himself more narrowly what precisely was the nature of the principle which he had adopted. By Imperialism he understood a free, informal union with the Colonies, combined with a conscientious but tolerant government of the tropical dependencies which have come under our control. But he has begun to realise that this was in essence the conception of the Empire bequeathed by the older generation of Liberals, and precisely the antithesis of present-day Imperialism, the operative principle of which is the forcible establishment and maintenance of racial ascendency. The central principle of Liberalism is self-government. The central principle of Imperialism, whatever words may be used to cloak it, is the subordination of self-government to Empire. The one stands for autonomy and the other for ascendency, and between these two ideas there can be no reconciliation, for they represent the most fundamental cleavage of political opinion. The trap laid for Liberals in particular consisted in this—that they were asked to give in their adhesion to Imperialism as representing admiration for an Empire which more and more has been shaped upon Liberal lines. Having given their assent, they were insensibly led on to the other meaning of Imperialism— a meaning in which, for all practical purposes, these principles are set aside. And there was a medium to facilitate the change. For if the Empire was so liberally formed, so free, tolerant, and unaggressive, could we have too much of it? Should we not extend its blessing to those that sit in darkness? And so, by a seductive blending of the old Adam of national vanity with the new spirit of humanitarian zeal men are led on to the destruction of their own principles.

Hitherto we have considered only the direct results of Imperialism. But its reaction on domestic politics is hardly less important. If

our "unprejudiced observer" was one of those
—and they were many—who, keenly desirous
of social progress, believed that the vigorous
forward action of the State in domestic
affairs would sort well with a similar
vigour and activity abroad, he has long
since found out his mistake. The dream
of combining a "spirited," that is in
reality an aggressive foreign policy with
domestic reform has melted away. The
absorption of public attention in foreign affairs
paralysed democratic effort at home. The worst
of Governments could always retain power by
raising the patriotic cry. Foreign complica-
tions proved unfavourable as ever to public
discussion, and the determination to rule others
had its normal effect on the liberties of the
ruling people themselves.

The growth of Imperialism has, in fact,
been one of those surprises which play ducks
and drakes with political prophecy. Both
the friends and enemies of democracy
inclined to the belief that when the people
came into power there would be a time of
rapid and radical domestic change combined
in all probability with peace abroad—for

where was the interest of the masses in any war? As it turned out, almost the first act of the new British democracy was to install the Conservatives in power, and to maintain them with but partial exceptions for nearly twenty years. Never were the fears or hopes of either side more signally disappointed. Before the event the advocates of popular government believed that they had now forged the necessary weapon of social advancement. There would be a new epoch of internal reform. Political democracy was in substance achieved, and the time was ripe for a series of social reforms which, in their aggregate effect, would amount to an even greater revolution. Industrial legislation of the type embodied in the Factory Acts would be perfected and extended to every occupation, so that short hours, healthy surroundings, and fair conditions should be the lot of every wage-earner. There would be compensation for all the accidents and diseases incident to industry, provision for sickness, and pensions for the aged. Municipalities, finally emancipated from the dominion of monopolist companies, and

endowed with new financial resources by
the taxation of immensely swollen land
values, would solve the housing question and
provide for sanitation, cleanliness, and public
recreation. The drink traffic, as the principal
source of demoralisation, would—no doubt
after a stiff fight—be brought under close
control, and therewith the problems of
pauperism and crime would be reduced to
manageable dimensions. Education, rendered
free, secular, and compulsory, would open
the best career for the best talents in every
class, while bodily raising all classes, including the lowest, in the scale of culture. Such
was the dream, and in many directions the
ablest men were giving their thoughts and
energy to its furtherance. The question how
to reorganise society as a democratic State,
not for a military but for an industrial life,
not in the two great classes of exploiters and
exploited but in an undivided community,
how to equalise opportunity, minimise the
causes of poverty, choke up the sources of
crime, in a word, how to realise the true
end of public and private ethics—the development of human faculty in orderly co-opera-

tion—such were the questions in which the best minds were absorbed, and which they believed would occupy the coming generation. In the light of the past ten years the bare statement reads like a satire on the vanity of human effort.

For social progress we have had out of the whole programme of the Nineties the partial fulfilment of one item—compensation for industrial accidents—to balance which we have had a reaction in finance, reviving a kind of class legislation supposed to be extinct, and a still more serious reaction in educational policy, threatening the definite reinstatement of clerical control. Lastly, as the outcome of two generations of temperance effort we have a measure aimed not at suppressing the temptations to drink, but at suppressing those magistrates who, with scanty powers, have done what in them lay to mitigate the evil, and entrenching the public-house behind the impregnable barrier of compensation. With this latest effort in social legislation the turning of the tables is indeed complete.

Here again it is not merely that mischievous and reactionary measures have been carried through, but that principles won by the sweat and blood of earlier generations have been lightly swept aside and methods introduced which threaten the very breath of our political life. Foremost among them stands the method of handing over public money or, what is the same thing, assigning relief from public burdens, first to one and then to another group of supporters of the Government in power. It is hardly possible under a popular suffrage to legislate in the interests of one class or one interest alone. But unfortunately a system of log-rolling is quite feasible, by which first one interest and then another gets "value received" for its political support, and the invention of this system is a heavy blow to popular government. And this is not the only blow that has fallen. On every side the popular element in our Constitution has been weakened and the elements of reaction have gathered strength. The House of Lords, once regarded as moribund, has shown itself capable of defeating Liberal legislation and reducing any democratic Government to

impotence and ineptitude. The Monarchy
—as the one realised flesh and blood bond of
union between all parts of the Empire—has
vastly increased its prestige, a change which,
whatever its immediate advantages when the
wearer of the crown happens to be wiser than
his constitutional advisers, can only be
viewed by men of popular sympathies with
grave concern for its ultimate outcome. The
House of Commons, meanwhile, in the
opinion of the best observers, has gradually
changed its character. It is ceasing to be
an arena for the full and free discussion of
public affairs, for the critical examination of
legislative proposals, and the ventilation of
public grievances. It is becoming more and
more a formal assemblage for the recognition
and registration of decisions taken by the
Executive, like the Homeric assembly to
which the chiefs announced their resolves.
Such has been the consequence on the one
hand of refusing Home Rule—another instance of the loss of our own liberties by
refusing liberty to others—on the other, of
the growth of business and preoccupation
with Imperial affairs, in which all the infor-

mation is in official hands and effective
criticism at the right moment is accordingly
a matter of extreme difficulty. Lastly, outside the sphere of politics proper the chief
working-class organisations, the Trade
Unions, have received a series of blows.
The position which Parliament undoubtedly
intended to give them and which they had
enjoyed for thirty years, has been revolu-
tionised by a sequence of judicial decisions,
which reflect—for judges, too, are human—
the changed temper of the time. The effect
is that this arm of the democratic movement
is for the moment paralysed.

Thus reaction at home is interwoven with
reaction abroad, and in the new principles we
see the whole circle of the Cobdenist ideas
turned, as it were, inside out. There we
saw that Free Trade, peace, retrenchment,
self-government, democratic progress were
mutually dependent principles. In their
reversal we see the same truth. Aggrandisement, war, compulsory enlistment, lavish
expenditure, Protection, arbitrary government, class legislation, follow naturally one
upon the other. They move along the same

line of thought, and the same lines of causal connection. But in proportion as that line has become clear and people have seen whither it would lead them, they have begun to doubt Imperialism. They have come to realise that the name stands, not for love of the Empire, but for the lust of Empire, not for the noble constitutional fabric built up by British energy and remodelled by the spirit of British liberty and fairdealing, but for the dream of conquest, the vanity of racial domination, and the greed of commercial gain.

CHAPTER III

THE political reaction briefly adverted to above is the expression of a far-reaching change in the temper of the time, which is by no means peculiar to our own country or to the sphere of politics. It is common to the civilised world, and penetrates every department of life and thought. If it is to be summed up in a word, we should call it a reaction against humanitarianism.

The sixty years which followed the Battle of Waterloo formed a period of fairly rapid social progress and of social progress correlated with an advance in social and moral science. Political enfranchisement, the reform of the Government services, Free Trade, the progressive regulation of the new industrial system, the abolition of negro slavery, the removal of the most barbarous features of the criminal law—these and many other reforms were all part of a great humanising movement stimulated and guided by the thought of the day. Not that any one thinker embraced or understood the whole movement. There were men like Carlyle, to whom anything like humanitarianism seemed mere sentimentality, but who, in spite of themselves, sympathised with certain sides of the onward movement, and did service in protesting against the too narrow interpretation of it by some of their contemporaries. But it is possible to characterise the thought of a generation without restricting one's view to a single thinker or a single school, and it is fair to say that the thought of the period in question was humanitarian—that is to say, it was concerned not merely with the direct alleviation of suffering and prevention of cruelty, but with the removal of fetters, the opening of opportunity to individual and national self-development, the utilisation of vastly increased material resources for the common benefit, the bringing in of the humblest to the banquet of civilisation. In a word, its governing principle was to deem those things best which do most to expand and further human life and happiness, and those things worst which do most to corrupt and destroy them. It was a movement of which the "Age of Reason" had dreamt, but for which it was inadequately equipped. The men of the nineteenth century knew more of history and more of the complexity of social cause and effect than their intellectual forbears. They were aware that a new Jerusalem could not be built in a day. Nevertheless, they held possible a progressive realisation of an ideal which could not be accomplished by a sudden political revolution. The rationalism which, in the previous century, had been Utopian, became in fact sober and more prosaic, but practical and progressive. The "ideas of '89" had been general and abstract, but the men of the period in question sought in very various ways, and no doubt with the usual amount of mutual misunderstanding and conflict, to give them concrete meaning and practical application.

Humanitarianism is now dismissed as

sentimentality. Its efforts at internationalism have yielded to a revival of national
exclusiveness, seen in the growth of armaments, the revival or aggravation of Protectionism, the growth of anti-alien legislation.
The doctrine of democratic rights has been
replaced by the demand for efficiency, or by
the unadorned gospel of blood and iron.
Indeed, the bare conception of right in
public matters has lost its force, and given
place to political "necessity" and "reasons
of State." Hence human wrongs and human
sufferings do not move us as they did.

Take as a single and sufficient illustration
of the change the question of slavery.
Nothing could be more characteristic of the
reaction than the general indifference to this
matter compared with the red-heat with
which our grandfathers discussed the question. Palmerston, for example, was one of
the last men to whom one would go for any
expression of humanitarian sentiment. Yet
this is how Palmerston, near the close of
his life, wrote about the slave trade :—

"During the many years that I was at the Foreign
Office there was no subject that more constantly or more

intensely occupied my thoughts, or constituted the aim of my labours; and though I may boast of having succeeded in accomplishing many good works . . . yet the achievement which I look back to with the greatest and purest pleasure was the forcing the Brazilians to give up their slave trade, by bringing into operation the Aberdeen Act of 1845." (Ashley's "Life," ii. p. 263.)

What, one wonders, would Palmerston have said to one of Sir A. Hardinge's despatches from East Africa with its contemptuous references to the "anti-slavery faction"? Thirty years ago the whole Empire was anti-slavery. Now, far from putting it down, we have on more than one occasion suffered the introduction of one form or other of servile labour under the British flag. It is difficult to conceive any great white nation waging war in these days on the slavery question. On the contrary, the prevailing, though perhaps veiled, opinion seems to be that the black or the yellow man must pay in meal or in malt for his racial inferiority. The white man is the stronger, and to the strong are the earth and the fruits thereof. If the black man owns land and lives on its produce, he is an idler. His "manifest destiny" is to assist in the development of gold mines for the benefit of humanity in general and the shareholders in particular.

The change of attitude towards slavery illustrates several features of the intellectual reaction. Partly it is traceable to want of concrete acquaintance with the thing itself. Our grandfathers were nearer to it, as they were nearer to a good many other political abuses. The principles of reform to which they appealed had a very real meaning to them in their struggle, just as at the present day personal liberty means more to a Russian or a South African than to an Englishman who has never known what it is to be without it. Many principles which they established we have let slip merely for want of imagination enough to realise what the denial of such principles would mean in practice.

Here we strike on one root of the reaction, the easygoing temper of the time—that temper which accepts the work of the past with a nod of recognition for its sacrifices, but, in comfortable assurance that the old troubles are done with, dismisses historical strife in the spirit of the Italian girl who, on being introduced to the ancient history of her country, protested that "these were very disagreeable people; they are all dead; let us hear no more about them." The easy materialism of our own time wanted to hear no more of principles in politics, and how they were endangered and how maintained. It had the results, and that was enough. The old battle-cries were flat and stale, and it would hear nothing of them that would conflict with the expediency of the moment. Prosperity and the political tranquillity achieved by the efforts of reformers had engendered a mood of scepticism.

This root of the intellectual reaction strikes deep into the social and political state of England. The energies of two generations of reformers have gone far to make the country satisfied with itself. "Never, perhaps, has there been material prosperity so widely diffused as in the last three or four years. While the rich have grown richer beyond the dreams of avarice, the poor have by no means grown poorer. Free trade, factory legislation, the vigorous development of Trade Unions, friendly societies, and co-

operative societies have not only increased
the aggregate amount of wealth in the
country, but have been the means of dis-
tributing it over wider and wider circles.
Old workmen who still remember the priva-
tions of the forties look on the present state
of their class as a paradise in comparison.
Along with this social progress the chief
political grievances have been abolished.
Though neither religious nor political nor
social nor economic inequalities have been
done away with, yet their burden is so far
lightened and so irregularly diffused that none
of them press on any part of the community
with such weight as to produce great sustained and widespread enthusiasm for their
removal. The pressure for further reform
among those who would most directly gain
by it has slackened.

"On the other hand, whole classes have
been won over definitely to the side of the
established order. The great middle class,
in particular, which seventy years ago was
knocking at the gates of political enfranchisement, now finds all the prizes and privileges
of public life open to its sons, the ablest of

whom crowd into the public services at home and abroad. If this favours Conservatism in general, it fosters Imperialism in particular, as was seen by Cobden nearly fifty years ago, when he wrote :—

" 'Nowhere has the [peace] movement fewer partisans than in Scotland, and the reason is obvious—first because your heads are more combative than even the English, which is almost a phrenological miracle ; and, secondly, the system of our military rule in India has been widely profitable to the middle and upper classes in Scotland, who have had more than their numerical proportion of its patronage. Therefore the military party is very strong in your part of the kingdom.' (Morley's 'Cobden,' ii. p. 144.)

" This would not have seemed out of place if written in 1902. But what was and is true of Scotland in particular is true of the middle classes generally. People talk much of the decay of Liberalism, and trace it, as is their wont, to this or that personal cause, but the great backward swing of the boroughs since 1868 is unmistakable, and its main cause is that Liberalism has done its work so thoroughly. The great middle class has become contented with its lot, and is far more moved by its fear of Socialism than by any desire for further instalments of privilege. In the old days it was outside the charmed circle, and thus naturally was all for reform; now it is sufficiently inside to get its share of warmth, and has more to fear from the widening of the circle than to hope from the more equal distribution of standing room within it. In particular it applauds the lead given it towards Imperialism. It applauds it in its capacity of respectable parent with sons to put out into the world, of merchant with trade to develop, of missionary with religion to push, above all of investor with capital to seek higher interest than can be gained at home. The true leaders of the middle class are the financiers, who show them how to get more than 3 per cent. on their investments, and as long as any man, English or German, Aryan or Semitic, will show them this, and throw an occasional cheque to a church or chapel, he may do what he pleases and snap his fingers at investigation.

" Conservatism, then, with a heavy Imperialistic bias, has, for political and economic reasons, taken a strong hold on the middle class, which a generation ago was the back-

bone of Liberalism. Owing to the very
success of Liberal efforts there has been a
great transfer of the material interests from
the reforming to the Conservative side. I
would not suggest that all ardour for political
and social justice is merely collective self-
interest. But it is probably true that people
who are denied justice themselves are more
ready to sympathise with others in the same
predicament, and more open to any appeal to
general principles. Those who have all they
want are far more disposed to believe that
God is in His heaven, and that there is
something wrong with those who cannot get
justice done to them. In these ways, without
taking a materialistic view of human motives,
it must be admitted that prosperity and full
political enfranchisément do tend to a form of
collective selfishness, and that in this lies
a real obstacle to the permanence of human
progress." *

* The above passage from an article written some two
years ago states, I think, fairly enough the political
conditions obtaining in the period before the Corn tax
and the Education Act. The further development of the
reaction since that time has at length aroused the artisans
and the more thoughtful of the middle class to a sense of

In our great middle class circumstances have contributed to foster collective selfishness. Suburban villadom is a political and social portent the meaning of which has never yet been fully analysed. All round every great centre is a ring of towns to which the men resort only to dine and sleep, while the women have no visible function in life except to marry and discuss marriages. While the private life of the suburb is no doubt comfortable and blameless, politically it is a greater burden on the nation than the slum. It has, to begin with, no healthy corporate life. Its menfolk are either engaged elsewhere and are too much exhausted by their own business to enter into local public life, or they are retired officers and civilians, residents whose only function is to reside. We have here a class of moderately well-to-do people almost wholly divorced from definite public duties— a class relatively new in this country. They are removed from contact with poverty or

public danger and to a fuller comprehension of the drift of the reaction. The consequence has been a counter-movement, through which the reaction has already received a check.

from any special obligation to any class of dependants. All they know of social and domestic reform is that it means expense, and their politics are summed up in the simple and comprehensive formula—keep down the rates. Imperialism is the only conception remotely related to an ideal which they comprehend, and if this too is expensive, we have seen that it offers them as a class ample compensation. Though elsewhere the middle class may be moved, it will be long before the big battalions of suburbia—accounting for no mean fraction of the electorate—will shift their ground. For here is a class educated, as education goes, too convinced of its own virtue and enlightenment to tolerate a prophet or a teacher, respectable to the point of being incapable of reform.

It would be a hopeless attempt to enumerate all the causes of the change in national temper, but that the nation has undergone such a change, and one that has struck its roots deep and wide into our life, can hardly be denied. The very figure of John Bull as the typical Englishman seems out of date and inapplicable as an expression for the average Briton of the present day. The easy-going, stout, well-meaning, rather dull old gentleman, a little proud if the truth be told of his very dulness, and apt to conceive of it as an incident in that fundamental honesty which distinguished him from his sharp-witted neighbours, the well-nourished territorial magnate, slow-going, hard to move, but implacable when once stirred, narrow perhaps, but fundamentally just and honourable in all his dealings, is no fit representative of the average public opinion of our day. For that, we have ourselves coined a new abstraction : * "the man-in-the-street," or the "man-on-the-top-of-a-bus" is now the typical representative of public opinion, and the man-in-the-street means the man who is hurrying from his home to his office, or to a place of amusement. He has just got the last news-sheet from his neighbour ; he has not waited to test or sift it ; he may have heard three contradictory reports, or seen two lying posters on his way up the street, but he has an ex-

---

* The Australians have invented a far more sinister term. For them John Bull-Cohen is now the impersonation of British Imperial policy.

pression of opinion ready on his lips, which is none the less confident, because all the grounds on which it is founded may be swept away by the next report that he hears. The man-in-the-street is the man in a hurry; the man who has not time to think and will not take the trouble to do so if he has the time. He is the faithful reflex of the popular sheet and the shouting newsboy. His character and the tone which he gives to our public discussions resemble more the character and tone which the proud and slow-going John Bull of old days was wont to attribute to his volatile and emotional neighbours who made revolutions and cut off the heads of kings, while he at home was priding himself on the slow and orderly march of reform. To this new public opinion of the streets and the tramcars it is useless to appeal in terms of reason; it has not time to put the two ends of an argument together; it has hardly patience to receive a single idea, much less to hold two in the mind and compare them. Equally futile is it to come before this tribunal with any plea for those higher con- siderations which men recognise in their quieter moods. Just as language is clipped and cut down in Cockney dialect, and educated conversation is debased into the common currency of street slang, so there is a kind of slang of ideas, a moral slang in which all the best thought of the world, the thought that needs unceasingly to be applied to public affairs, gets clipped and chopped up and debased till all the strength has evaporated from it. The man-in-the-street is familiar with everything. Nothing is new to him; it is his business not to be surprised. He knows already all about any appeal that you can make to the better side of him, and he has long ago chopped it up in his mill of small talk and catch phrases and reduced it to such a meaningless patter that the words which must be used have acquired trivial and lowering associations. It used to be thought that education would open men's minds to the conceptions necessary for the new masters of the State, but education itself must in large measure be ranked among our failures. When our higher education has such dismal results, what are we to expect from the mechanical training

in the elements of learning which is all that
we are able to give to the public at large?
Properly speaking, we have no educated
classes; we have numerous men and women
who in spite of the schools have educated
themselves. But those who most stoutly
defend the great public schools in which
the majority of the governing classes spend
their boyhood, seldom do so on the ground
of the actual teaching which these schools
confer; they lay stress on the gains for social
life, the hardening elements—so necessary
for " re-barbarisation "—the plan of making
a boy fend for himself from a very early
age, but they seldom pretend that the actual
teaching has any measurable effect except
upon a small minority. In point of fact
the net result of the years spent upon Latin
and Greek seems to be to alienate the mind
from the study of literature, and to cultivate
a taste for anything rather than the Classics.
Any education is probably better than none,
since even the worst teaching has the effect
of training the mind to work, and so grow,
like a muscle, by exercise. But of real
mental training, of stimulus to the imagina-

tion, of cultivation of the reasoning powers, of any endeavour to suggest a wide rational human outlook upon the problems of life, there is little question.

That the people as a whole have learnt to read has no doubt had the result that a certain portion of them have read the literature that is worth reading. Another result has been that the output of literature that is not worth reading has vastly increased. Once again, to suit the man-in-the-street, everything must be chopped up into the smallest possible fragments to assist digestion; even the ordinary article of the old journalism has proved far too long and too heavy; it must be cut up into paragraphs, punctuated by frequent spaces, and spiced with epigrammatic absurdities to catch attention on the wing. It must be diversified with headlines and salted with sensationalism; if it is to sell, it must appeal to the uppermost prejudices of the moment. As to news, mere fidelity to fact ceases to be of moment when everything is forgotten within twenty-four hours, and when people do not really read in order that they may know, but in order that their attention may be momentarily diverted from the tedium of the train or the tramcar. Such a public may be swayed by pity, as by other obvious and easy emotions, provided no prejudice stands in the way of its humanity, but for the most part it takes its daily toll of bloodshed in the news paragraphs as a part of the diurnal repast, and if there were no real wars, murders or sudden deaths, would probably expect the enterprising journalist to invent them. A big battle in the Far East, or the slaughter of a few hundred primitively-armed Tibetans is a pleasing pendant to the narration of athletic contests, in which harmless direction this public fortunately finds its principal entertainment. It is, of course, the athletic and sporting news which in the main sells the papers in the streets. The marvellous diffusion of interest in these matters, while a result of the general growth of material prosperity, is also a bar to the maintenance of any wide-spread interest in public affairs. It would be difficult to find any question of politics or social welfare, or even of religion, which would attract a Lancashire crowd

such as will flock to the Yorkshire match,
or to imagine any public boon which would
stir emotions so wide and deep as would
be raised by the news of another " century "
by Tyldesley. No social revolution will come
from a people so absorbed in cricket and
football. Should the beginnings of a movement appear, society has an easy way of
dealing with it. In old days they hanged
the leaders of popular movements. Now
they ask them to dinner—a method of
painless extinction which has proved far
more effective.

The mention of religion leads us naturally
to the consideration of the causes of this
change in the national temper; among these,
the decay in vivid and profound religious
beliefs must certainly hold a place. This
decay was in process a generation ago, but
its effects at that time were off-set by the
rise of a humanitarian feeling which, partly
in alliance with the recognised Churches,
and partly outside them, took in a measure
the place of the old convictions, supplying
a stimulus and a guidance to effort and
yielding a basis for a serious and rational

public life. But the promises of that time
have not been fulfilled. Humanitarianism,
as we have seen, has lost its hold, and the
resulting temper is a good-natured scepticism,
not only about the other world, but also
about the deeper problems and higher interests of this world.

The prevailing temper has, as is its wont,
fashioned for itself a theory. Indeed it has
found more than one theory ready to serve
it. It can found itself on the current
philosophy, on recent political history, and on
the supposed verdict of physical science.

The most popular philosophy of our time
has had a reactionary influence, the
extent of which is perhaps not generally
appreciated. For thirty years and more
English thought has been subject, not for
the first time in its modern history, to powerful influences from abroad. The Rhine has
flowed into the Thames, at any rate into
those upper reaches of the Thames, known
locally as the Isis, and from the Isis the
stream of German idealism has been diffused
over the academical world of Great Britain.
It would be natural to look to an idealistic

philosophy for a counterpoise to those crude
doctrines of physical force which we shall
find associated with the philosophy of
science. Yet, in the main, the idealistic
movement has swelled the current of retrogression. It is itself, in fact, one expression
of the general reaction against the plain,
human, rationalistic way of looking at life
and its problems. Every institution and
every belief is for it alike a manifestation
of a spiritual principle, and thus for everything there is an inner and more spiritual
interpretation. Hence, vulgar and stupid
beliefs can be held with a refined and enlightened meaning, known only to him who
so holds them, a convenient doctrine for
men of a highly-rarefied understanding, but
for those of coarser texture who learn from
them apt to degenerate into charlatanism.
Indeed, it is scarcely too much to say that
the effect of idealism on the world in general
has been mainly to sap intellectual and
moral sincerity, to excuse men in their
consciences for professing beliefs which on
the meaning ordinarily attached to them
they do not hold, to soften the edges of all

hard contrasts between right and wrong, truth and falsity, to throw a gloss over stupidity, and prejudice, and caste, and tradition, to weaken the bases of reason, and disincline men to the searching analysis of their habitual ways of thinking.

In these ways idealism has had a more subtly retrograde influence than any of the cruder scientific creeds which it condemns, and has thus prepared the way for the scepticism which has been the popular philosophy of the last ten years. To judge by the popularity of teaching of this kind, what people who think a little mainly want at the present day is to be told that they need not follow where their own reason takes them. There is, they are glad to be assured, no logical foundation for the certainty which the sciences claim. Still less is there any rational groundwork of morality, in particular for that humanitarian morality, which they have found so exacting. They can, there-fore, with a lightened intellectual conscience revert to the easy rule of authority and faith, a rule particularly attractive to a society which has become afraid of further progress and is lusting after the delights of barbarism.

The trend of events has appeared on the surface to justify these philosophic doubts of humanitarian duty. Hegelianism had its political sponsor in Bismarck, and Hegel's teaching, apart from that subtler influence upon thought which I have attempted to characterise, had a distinct bearing upon political questions which was upon the whole reactionary. For him, the ideals of the eighteenth century on which, say what we may, political Liberalism is founded, were merely a phase in the negative movement of thought, a phase which his higher synthesis was definitely to overcome. They belonged to the kind of rationalism with which Hegel had no sympathy, being convinced that he had found out a more excellent way. In place of the rights of the individual Hegel set the State—and for him the State was not to serve humanity, but was an end in itself. It was not to serve the Church, nor even to be separate from the Church; on the contrary, the modern State was to be the fountain of religious as well as secular

authority. It summed up in itself both the
temporal and the spiritual order. Clearly,
then, there were no limits to its authority,
nor was there any necessary responsibility on
the part of its Government. At any rate, an
absolute monarch might express the popular
will quite as well as a democratic Parliament.
Bismarck's career was a concrete exemplifica-
tion of the Hegelian State,* crushing out
popular resistance, and in relation to other
States a law to itself. Bismarck first showed
the modern world what could be done in the
political sphere by the thorough-going use of
force and fraud. The prestige of so great an
apparent success naturally compelled imita-
tion, and to the achievements of Bismarck,
as we are dealing with the forces which have
moulded opinion in our own day, we must
add the whole series of trials in which the
event has apparently favoured the methods
of blood and iron, and discredited the cause
of liberty and justice. The spectacle of the

* The Bismarckian theory and its relation to Hegel-
ianism are admirably analysed in an article by the late
Mr. William Clarke in the *Contemporary Review* for
January, 1899.

Turkish Sultan persisting in a long series of massacres with absolute impunity could not fail to affect opinion. On the other side, the new nations, whose rise had been witnessed with so much enthusiasm by the friends of liberty throughout the nineteenth century, turned out, it must be confessed, a disappointment in our own time. The spectacle of Italy using her regained liberty to build up a great military power upon the sufferings of her people, and to embark upon a policy of aggression utterly unsuited to her genius, was sufficiently chilling to the ardour of men brought up on the teachings of Mazzini.* The overthrow of Greece was a minor instance of the same tendency. In every direction there was disappointment for those who identified liberty with national self-government, while there was everything to encourage men prone to be impressed by force, order, discipline, and the setting of national efficiency above freedom. Of course,

---

* Conversely, the quite recent revival of Italy is a new augury of hope, which may be set side by side with the check to militarism in France and the Liberal-Labour revival in England.

to those who looked deeper, much of Bismarck's work was evidently hollow. He might create an army and an Empire, but he could not give back to Germany the days of Kant, of Goethe, of Fichte and of Schelling. The only vital force in Germany is a revolutionary force. Apart from social democracy—which is driven by the Government into a revolutionary attitude—there is in Germany to-day none of that spiritual energy by which in the past Germany has inspired the world. It is true German specialism is a power, and the weight of German learning has had an effect on thinking people all the world over. But it is precisely the vice of modern German thought that it is specialism. It is learning divorced from its social purpose, destitute of large and generous ideas, worse than useless as a guide in the problems of national life, smothering the humanities in cartloads of detail, unavoidable, but fatal to the intellect. In the Germanisation of the intellectual world we see the reason why the advance of knowledge has borne as yet so little fruit or life.

But after all, by far the most potent

intellectual support of the reaction has been neither the idealistic philosophy nor the impression made by contemporary events, but the belief that physical science had given its verdict in favour—for it came to this— of violence and against social justice.

I spoke above of slavery, and how it seemed to our grandfathers a denial of the fundamental rights of humanity. But the question is raised by the current interpretation of biological science whether humanity has any fundamental rights at all. If our grandfathers declared that the black man was a man and a brother, our generation replied that he is but the son of the bond woman, born to be a hewer of wood and drawer of water to the stronger race; and far from seeing any immorality in this arrangement, the prevalent theory is that it is by adding strength to the strong, by giving to them that have, and taking from them that have not, that the fittest survives and the race improves.

The doctrine that human progress depends upon the forces which condition all biological evolution has in fact been the primary intellectual cause of the reaction. Just as the doctrine of Malthus was the main theoretical obstacle to all schemes of social progress through the first two-thirds of the century, so the doctrine derived in part from Malthus by Darwin has provided a philosophy for the reaction of the last third.   Darwin himself, indeed, was conscious of the limitations of his own hypothesis, and was aware that the development of the moral consciousness in man involves from the first a suspension of the blind struggle for existence.   But those who have applied Darwin's theories to the science of society have not as a rule troubled themselves to understand Darwin any more than the science of society.   What has filtered through into the social and political thought of the time has been the belief that the time-honoured doctrine " Might is Right " has a scientific foundation in the laws of biology.   Progress comes about through a conflict in which the fittest survives.   It must, therefore, be unwise in the long run— however urgent it seems for the sake of the present generation—to interfere with the struggle.   We must not sympathise with the beaten and the weak, lest we be tempted

to preserve them. The best thing that can
happen is that they should be utterly cut off,
for they are the inferior stock, and their blood
must not mix with ours. The justice, the
mercy, the chivalry, which would induce the
conqueror to forbear from enjoying the full
fruits of his victory must be looked on with
suspicion. It is better to smite the Amalek-
ite hip and thigh and let the conquering
race replenish the earth.

By its most logical exponents, this conception is applied to the relations of individuals in society, but so applied it is readily
seen to involve a mere denial of the value of
social order, every advance in which involves
a further suspension of the struggle for
existence. Bagehot, I believe, was the first
to point out that it might as readily be
applied to nations, and that human progress
might be thought of as resting on the struggle
not of individuals but of communities. Thus
conceived the theory has somewhat anoma-
lous results. Internal peace, harmony, and
justice, with all the moral qualities which
they imply, are readily recognised as necessary
to national efficiency, but as between nations

these principles cease to apply. If it is the business of the individual to be a loyal and law-abiding subject of the State, it is the business of the State merely to advance itself and trample down all who cross its path. The rule of right, it appears, stops short at the frontier. It hardly seems to need arguing that this is not in the end a tenable view. It is safe to say that the conduct of a State and its external relations must react upon its internal character, and the negation of a principle in one relation must affect its authority in others. If the morality which applies to individuals does not apply to the State, why does it apply to any other association—a family, a church, a trade union ? But if it does not apply to such associations, and if those who act for them are not to be held morally accountable, there is an end to the ethical basis of that very social order which was admitted to be necessary.*

Not only the central conception of the biological theory of society, but its secondary and consequential doctrines, have militated

---

* I recur to this particular aspect of the question below, Chap. viii.

as though by a perverse fatality against social justice. The very belief in race and the value of inheritance are hostile in tendency to social reform. No doubt the old reformers, with their belief in the almost indefinite modifiability of mankind, were a great deal too sanguine as to what could be effected by a change of institutions, but at least the exaggeration had in practice a stimulating effect. Believing in improvement, they attempted to improve, whereas for those who believe that improvement takes place only through physiological laws, which at any rate for the present are far beyond our control, there is no purpose to be achieved by a reform of institutions. The tendency of this line of thought is to fall back upon the good old maxim that each should improve himself. The value of the individual, or more strictly, the value of the breed, is for it the one point of fundamental importance, and it holds that whatever temporary improvement is achieved by other methods, if the strain itself is not purified, there will be a relapse, and possibly worse than a relapse. Hence from Malthus downwards stress on

the biological conditions of society has naturally been associated with a bias towards
conservatism.

Conversely the doctrine of equality is a
natural basis for social and political reform.
As a matter of fact this doctrine is not
touched by biological theory. No doubt it
is capable of being stated in a form which
ignores differences in the capacities of mankind—though, to be perfectly just, it must
be admitted that such statements have more
often been put into the mouths of the upholders of equality by their opponents, who
have wished to put the theory in a form
which it was easy to confute—but, however
perverted, the doctrine of equality lends
itself naturally to doctrines of social, national,
sexual and racial justice. In such doctrines
the fundamental fact about the human being
is that he is a human being and enjoys
accordingly certain fundamental rights. The
announcement of this view in the modern
world amounted to a revolution, because it
found society based on distinctions of class,
of sex and of colour, which implied a denial
of these fundamental rights. Now the bio-

logical theory has re-introduced these differences and imparted to them a certain scientific
air. The black man, the biologist points out,
is not in point of fact the equal of the white
man in mental and moral capacity. He has
been the subject of a different evolution. He
has grown up in a distinctive environment,
with the result that he has evolved differences
of quality, moral and intellectual, as well as
physical, and you may as well deny that he
is black as assert that he is equally capable
of civilisation with his white master. In
strictness, this argument is quite irrelevant to
a doctrine which does not allege that men
are equal, but that law and institutions should
treat them equally, or in other words, should
make between them only such differences as
they merit by their own actions. Nevertheless, the biological conception, working upon
an easy confusion of ideas, has led to a disintegration of the painfully reared fabric of
humanitarian justice, playing into the hands
of what is called the relative, and sometimes
the historical, view of right and wrong, giving
a semblance of reason to the contention that
we should treat different beings differently;

that the institutions for which the white man has fitted himself, being the result of a special evolution, are not fitted for the black, and that we should accordingly in dealing with him adapt our own institutions to his accustomed environment. Scientific as this sounds, it means in practice that when the white man comes into contact with lower civilisations, he should lower himself to their level. The black man, for example, is accustomed to slavery, and the only conclusion of the argument is that the white man may justly preserve this institution for the common benefit. The flaw in this argument is first that it lays down an inequality of endowments and proceeds therefrom to a denial of equal rights. Secondly, those who use it do not carry their inquiries far enough. Content to establish the general fact of inequality, they do not stay to inquire into its nature and degree, still less to prove that it justifies the arbitrary treatment which they uphold. Thus, to keep to the question of slavery as a test, the Kaffir is after all a human being, if an inferior, and when his case is enquired into dispassionately, it seems that in relation to labour he is after all animated by very much the same motives as other human beings. He is not, it is true, particularly fond of work, but he works when the necessity of living compels him to do so, and he goes by preference where he can get the best wages and enjoy the best conditions. In all this he bears a striking family resemblance to the white man or the yellow man or any other member of this imperfect species.* That being so, one fails to see why the well-recognised economic motives which appeal to the white—good wages and fair conditions for example—should not appeal with equal

* See the admirable remarks of Sir Marshall Clark (Correspondence on Native Labour in Rhodesia, 1902) : "The true inducement to labour, and the only one, I submit, calculated to benefit the natives is the development of legitimate wants which money can satisfy;" and again, "Some few mines and employers have earned for themselves a bad reputation. But this is soon brought home to them by the difficulty they experience in obtaining and keeping natives to work—a natural result, by no means the least advantage derived from free labour." The advocate of native rights is always being told that he is a sentimentalist who knows nothing of the men about whom he is talking. Yet, when an expert speaks who happens to view the native not merely as a "living implement" but as a human being, he is found on the side of the sentimentalist.

force to the Kaffir, and it requires a much more thorough investigation of the subject at the hands of much less prejudiced observers than those who wish to exploit his labour, to convince the onlooker that any departure from equality of treatment is justified under this head. A just application of evolutionary principles to the governing of less civilised races will doubtless entail certain differences in the treatment accorded to them, but unfortunately it is precisely this just application which, in the present temper of the governing race, whose material interests are so much involved, we can hardly hope to see.

Lastly, in a more general sense, the theory of evolution has led to a kind of fatalism, which consorts well with the materialist principles which have become popular. Evolution is conceived as a vast world process in which human will and human intelligence play a subordinate, and, in a sense, blind and unconscious part. The great biological forces work themselves out without any conscious contribution from the organisms with which they sport. Humanity is a product of forces similar in character to those which made the ape, and, for that matter, the oyster. It does not shape its own fate. The most intelligent actions, the widest schemes, the noblest ideals of men are produced by physical causes of which they are unconscious, and have biological effects which bear no relation to the intentions of the agent concerned. The future of society is not in the hands of statesmen or thinkers, but is determined by the play of forces which are beyond human control. It can be ascertained by science and predicted by biological writers on human society who are adequately furnished with a distinct conception of our manifest destiny. That that manifest destiny has a strong tendency to fall in with the prevailing mood of the day, is an accident, perhaps a happy accident for the biological writers. But be that as it may, these writers find in manifest destiny an excuse for the doing of things by society as a whole, which would be ethically reprehensible if done by any other human association. For by the conception of destiny the check on the moral consciousness is paralysed. It is useless to fight against fate. If it is our destiny to become masters of the earth let us surrender ourselves, they say, to the forces which urge us on, and which in the past made our fathers build better than they knew. Great empires advance, they say, not so much by express intention and through the designing policy of individuals, as by a kind of blind impulse, urging them on, they know not how or why, forcing them from step to step till they find themselves in a position quite remote from anything they set out to attain. Against this stony fatalism the sense of justice cries out in vain.

Thus in diverse forms and sundry manners the belief that success is its own justification has penetrated the thought of our time. At one time the appeal is to destiny, at another to natural selection, at a third to the inequalities implanted by heredity, at yet another to the demonstrated efficiency of blood and iron. The current of thought has joined that of class interest, and the united stream sweeps onward in full flood to the destruction of the distinctive landmarks of modern civilised progress.

CHAPTER IV

EVOLUTION AND SOCIOLOGY

WE have thus traced the Reaction on its intellectual side to the biological conception of Evolution as its principal source. We have roughly indicated fallacious elements in this conception, but it will be well to discuss it a little more fully, and consider whether a truer theory may not be found to take its place.

The theory that human progress depends on the struggle for existence claims recognition as a scientific truth. But though a theory of the progress of society, we do not find that it is based on the science of society. On the contrary we always find in discussing it that we are dealing with purely biological arguments drawn from observation of the plant and animal kingdom.

The biological view is that since men are
animals the laws regulating human development must be identical with those which we
observe in the breeding of shorthorns or of
fan-tailed pigeons. The pigeon-fancier should,
it appears, have more to teach us of the
conditions of human progress than Gibbon or
Mommsen. It is worth remarking that this
is a view against which great sociologists like
Comte warned us long ago. Every higher
and more special science is in part dependent
on those which are lower and more general.
Thus it is certainly true that, man being an
animal, every science that deals with man
must take account of the results ascertained
by biology as the general science of life.
Psychology, for example, must start furnished
with all that biology can teach of the structure
and function of brain and nerve. Similarly,
biology itself, since it deals with organised
matter, must learn from physics and chemistry
what they have to teach about the behaviour
of matter in general and of the specific
substances found in organised bodies in
particular. But when the biologist comes to
deal with the actual behaviour of organic

matter in the living organism, he is by no means disposed to let the physicist or chemist dogmatise as to what he must find. On the contrary he knows what he himself finds by his own methods, and this is often enough the very opposite of what pure physics would lead him to expect. The higher science, in fact, though dependent on the lower, ought by no means to merge its identity therein. This loss of identity Comte called materialism, because it hands over the higher, more complex, more subtle things of the world to be dealt with by methods appropriate to things of a coarser texture. It puts the living on a level with the inanimate, and the higher life with the lower. This lapse into materialism is precisely what has befallen the science of society in our own time. Volumes are written on sociology which take no account of history, no account of law, nor of ethics, nor of religion, nor of art, nor of social relations in their actual development, and, above all, have no consistent standard of value by which to measure the progress of which they speak. And their utterances are held to be the verdict of " science," to which the mere student of society must yield.

That the biologist should have no standard of value is perfectly natural. He is concerned with life, with structure and function, with organisation in all its forms. He traces the evolution of the simpler into the more complex, of the general into the special, without asking or needing to ask whether one form is higher or lower than another. But he does make one general assumption. If one form supersedes another it is because it is better adapted to the conditions of existence. The ichthyosaurus or the dodo have died out because they were comparatively ill-adapted to maintain themselves. They made room for creatures better organised for that supreme purpose. And the same process it is assumed goes on in human society. The ill-adapted perish while the fitter survive.

So far we are on firm ground, but a danger arises when fitness to survive is taken as evidence of superiority in other respects. As long as we think of life only as an end there can be no question of any other kind of fitness, and this is precisely the biological view. But if we conceive of one kind of life as intrinsically higher than another, and ask whether the type best fitted to survive is necessarily the type best adapted to that higher life, a perfectly new question arises to which the biologist as such is not equipped with any answer. For in the struggle of the organic world there is not the smallest reason to think that the survivor is naturally the " higher " in any sense except that he is best adapted for that struggle. If there is such a distinction as higher and lower at all, it will be admitted that human beings are higher organisms than microbes. Yet to this day many disease germs wage no unequal struggle with the lords of creation, while in the past they have frequently swept off whole populations. The tubercle, in fact, is better fitted to survive than the consumptive patient whom it infests. But we should not on that account call it a higher organism. Nor does the evolution which the struggle to maintain itself involves of necessity lead the organism from a lower to a higher type. If there is any meaning in the terms the parasite is a lower being than the host which it besets. Yet a vast variety of parasites are degenerate forms of organisms previously adapted to an independent life. Finally, a whole sub-kingdom, the Protozoa, has been left by all the geologic periods substantially in the same unicellular form of organisation from which the ancestors of the " highest " animals are presumed to have started, and in that form it maintains itself as vigorously as ever.

In a word, there is no inherent " upward " tendency in evolution so far as it is dependent on the struggle for existence. Old types may be maintained, or new types may arise, but there is nothing to determine whether the new will or will not be capable of a life fuller and better worth having than the old. The point is of first-rate importance in judging of the use of biological analogies in the science of society. The justification of any breach of ethics by the " laws of evolution " ceases to be valid as soon as it is understood that those " laws " have no essential tendency to make for human progress.

If we are to apply evolutionary theory to the science of society we must begin by defining our terms. The whole course of

organic evolution has sometimes been compared to a tree. From the parent stock—the
lowest organic type—branches spring out in all
directions, and form the different classes and
orders of the animal and vegetable kingdom.
We may for our purposes treat one of these
branches—that which leads to the sub-kingdom of Vertebrates, and thereby to the
Mammals, the Primates, and finally to Man—
as the main ascending trunk, and speak of
organisms as higher or lower according to the
position they occupy on this line of development. We can justify this use of terms if
we agree that mind is higher than matter, and
the more developed mind than the less developed. We have then a distinct criterion
of higher and lower, and shall know what
we mean when we say that the higher type
comes into being or survives. We shall
recognise also that it is only evolution along
the main or ascending line that we need care
about, evolution in other directions being
indifferent or worse. To this evolution of the
main stem the name of orthogeny or orthogenic evolution has been given, and this being
understood, we may say that on a scientific

theory of society progress should be determined not by the conditions of evolution in general, but by the distinctive requirements of orthogenic evolution as opposed to any other possible evolution.

If orthogenic evolution consists in the expansion of mind, how are we to measure this expansion, and what can we say of its results? From the point of view of the evolutionist, which for the moment we are taking up, mind is to be treated primarily as a factor in evolution, and mind becomes a factor in evolution in so far as it determines the behaviour of the individual, and thereby the life and development of the species. An animal gives evidence of intelligence in so far as it can be shown to utilise experiences for the achievement of purposes, and we may even measure mental development by the clearness and comprehensiveness with which the teaching of experience is grasped, and the scope and elevation of the purposes pursued. In the lowest orders of animal organisms the evidence of intelligence as measured by this test reaches a vanishing-point. The behaviour of the animal is

not guided by the teachings of its own
experience, but by the most elementary
forms of "instinct." Instinct comparative
psychology teaches us to regard as behaviour
based on the structure which the organism
inherits from its ancestors, and which acts in a
sense mechanically when the appropriate touch
or stimulus is supplied by some outer object.

Half or wholly mechanical reactions un-
informed by intelligence are probably all that
the lowest organisms * have for the guidance
of their behaviour. But far down in the
animal kingdom a new factor appears in the
capacity of the animal to modify its behaviour
in accordance with the results of its experience. This capacity appears at first to be

---

* Their character is best understood by thinking of
one of the many instances of mechanical reaction which
remain among men. A familiar one is the act of
blinking when something appears to threaten the eyes.
The closing of the eyelids serves to protect the eye, but
we do not close them deliberately with that object. They
close themselves in a mechanical fashion, which, as every
one knows, we find it hard to prevent if we try. Our
inherited physical structure provides this mechanism for
the protection of the eye, operating without the aid of
intelligence. The "instinctive" behaviour of a lower
animal is of the same general character.

limited to very simple cases, the range of intelligence not extending beyond the immediate consequences of the act or impulse.* But, still within the animal world, there comes a stage at which remoter consequences may be anticipated and steps taken to provide for them, as when a dog checks the impulse of the moment in fear of subsequent punishment. But throughout the animal world the main lines of behaviour are laid down by the blindly-acting inherited structure which we call instinct, and intelligence is applied mainly in rendering the plan of instinct more elastic, and adapting it to cases for which a fixed mechanical structure could not provide. In the human world this is changed. Each child is born not only with its own inherited faculties and impulses which correspond to animal instinct, but into a society with rules of life inherited in a different sense, handed on by tradition. The individual has neither to puzzle out his own rule of life, nor yet is it fixed for

---

* A chick which has pecked at a piece of orange peel and apparently, as its gestures indicate, found it disagreeable, will avoid orange peel thereafter, while it will peck with increased avidity at the yolk of egg which suits its cannibal tastes.

him by his instincts, but it is in large measure
laid down for him in its main lines in the
rules of art or handicraft, the code of law,
ethics, and religion, recognised by the community into which he is born. Thus so far as
these social traditions are the work of intelligence, it may be said that in the human
world intelligence has replaced instinct as
the guide of life not merely in incidental
actions but in the main lines of conduct.

But, of course, in the original formation of
social traditions it is only in a very blind and
halting way that intelligence operates, and
we must recognise the contributory, perhaps
the dominating influence of factors that are
not intelligent at all, emotions and prejudices,
hopes and fears, egotisms and antipathies
which clothe themselves in strange forms, and
give to the religion and morals of the natural
man a strangely mottled aspect of good and
evil elements. But as the mind comes to
itself and learns to measure its capacities and
use its powers there is a gradual purging of
the code. There is an attempt to go below
the surface, to go back from the rules which
men repeat and hand on to the principle

which underlies and justifies them, and the great religious and ethical systems are born. Since all these systems aim at a rational guidance of life towards some end which, whether supernatural or secular, is conceived as the highest object of human endeavour, their rise must be regarded as a great step forward in the direction of life by intelligent reflection. From the evolutionist point of view they are, in fact, successful in proportion as they tend to bring human faculty to the fulness of its development, and make the mind of man mistress of itself and its environment.

And it is towards this end that in the higher societies ethico-religious teaching moves. The primitive divisions of class, caste, race, or nationality are replaced by the conception of humanity as a whole, the arbitrary and irrational elements which survive from primitive custom are shed, and the conception of duty becomes remodelled on the basis of a rational understanding of the actual needs of individual and social life. The idea of personal salvation, in which social duty plays a subordinate part, is merged in a conception of social justice with reference to which personal duty is principally determined. In these and other ways, too numerous even for brief reference in this place, there arises by degrees the ideal of collective humanity, self-determining in its progress, as the supreme object of human activity, and the final standard by which the laws of conduct should be judged. The establishment of such an ideal, to which as a fact the historical development of the moral consciousness points, is the goal to which the mind, in its effort to master the conditions of existence, necessarily strives, and all the previous stages of mental evolution may be regarded as marking steps in the movement to this end.

Orthogenic evolution then is conceived as a process in which the control of the conditions of life gradually passes to that intelligence which in its lowest stages is the merest fleck of foam upon the waters which roll the life of the organic creation hither and thither as they list. This change, infinitely slow as it may be, constitutes the onward movement of humanity. Two of its results call for our attention here, one positive and one negative.

The positive result is that whether we treat it as biologists, psychologists, or sociologists, that is to say, whether we compare physical organisms, mental characters, or social institutions, the growth of mind implies always advance of organisation, and advance of organisation depends on the two principles —at first sight opposed—of unity and differentiation. The actual physical organisation which conditions mental growth in the individual will best illustrate what I mean. In animals of low organisation the different parts of the body are so loosely connected as to be in a measure independent of one another. Divide the animal in the proper manner, and you may make of it two, three, or perhaps more separate animals, each quite capable of an independent existence. In some cases the separation often takes place in the natural course, and the observer has difficulty in determining whether he is really dealing with one living being which can easily be divided, or with a number which congregate and act together. Here, then, is a lack of the organic unity which among ourselves binds the whole and parts so closely together. Between the

two extremes are many degrees which need
not be specified here. But it should be said
that the lower organism, besides being less
closely knit together, is also less differentiated.
In each several part very nearly the same
structure is repeated, and this is really the
reason why each part is capable of independent life. In us, on the other hand, with a
close-knit unity there is also a thoroughgoing
differentiation of structure.

Passing from the physical to the mental
we have seen that the growth of mind may
be measured by its capacity to utilise experience and direct action towards an end.
This is a second kind of organisation which
we may call indifferently the organisation of
experience or of conduct. In the lowest
grades we have seen that a germinating
intelligence may check or discourage a particular impulse, but can hardly advance to the
intelligent ordering of distinct acts. So far
as intelligence is concerned life is not yet
organised towards any distinct end. At a
higher stage we saw that the remoter consequences of an act might come into consideration, and so far actions become more

ordered and consecutive. At the same grade interest in other beings arises. There is evidence of care for the young, for a master, for an animal friend, and so far as this affection extends there is co-operation, and that again is a third kind of organisation. The efforts of different individuals play into one another. In the human world this kind of organisation is developed into a social order maintained and regulated by traditional ideas. Here the two conditions by which we measure organisation reappear under the familiar names of order and liberty. In the lowest societies custom is tyrannical, and there is little scope for individual divergences from the normal type, yet the conception of a common good is narrow and the means of maintaining order small. In the higher society the requirements of the common good are supreme, yet the establishment of civil order gives more free play to individuality. Civilisation is distinguished from barbarism, not more by the order which it establishes than by the many-sided development which it allows. Primitive life, though less orderly, is more monotonous, while the highest ideals, which enable us best to see life as a whole, reveal it as a "dome of many-coloured glass," not "staining" but rather reflecting, in the richness of human individuality and with the warmth of free, spontaneous, original impulse, the " white radiance " of eternal truth.

These commonplaces may suffice to illustrate what is meant by "higher" and "lower" organisation, and how the higher, whether physically, mentally, or sociologically considered, is always that in which a richer, fuller, more differentiated structure is knitted together in a deeper, more thoroughgoing unity. So far for the positive quality of "higher" organisation. The negative aspect is not less important for our purpose. The advance of organisation diminishes the opportunities for conflict. In proportion as life is well ordered the struggle for existence is suppressed. Biologists have seen in this a ground for apprehending that efforts towards social reform must necessarily defeat themselves, because the milder manners of civilised society and the multiplication of beneficent institutions preserve individuals who in a ruder age would have succumbed. Thus inferior stocks, which natural selection would weed out, are allowed to perpetuate themselves, and the race deteriorates. But the truth is that all orthogenic evolution, from the lowest organisms upwards, involve the progressive curtailment of the struggle for existence. The lowest organisms have an extraordinarily high rate of multiplication. A single pair— or rather, as generation is here a-sexual, a single organism—would have many million, even in some cases many billion, of descendants in a few months if these were allowed to multiply unchecked. But as under normal circumstances no such rapid increase takes place, it follows that the vast majority of the young are extirpated before they reach maturity. That is to say, that in the lowest grades of life there is on the average only one survivor out of potential millions. So intense is this struggle for existence, and so vast the field within which "natural selection" can be exercised. As we ascend the animal kingdom we find that, notwithstanding fluctuations due to other causes, in the main the rate of multiplication gradually declines. The highest mammals are the slowest breeders, and man, with perhaps one exception the slowest of all, multiplies and covers the earth notwithstanding. Taking the animal world as a whole, then, we must conclude that the lower the species the keener the struggle for existence, a generalisation which is fatal to the opinion of biologists that the struggle for existence is the condition of progress.

At every stage the struggle for existence is further curtailed by civilisation. With comparatively few exceptions, savages live in small communities in which the state of war may be said to be normal, while blood-feuds between families or clans are of constant recurrence. Yet it is precisely the savage who has not progressed. It is strange that biologists do not realise the bearing of this fact. Thus Professor Karl Pearson writes : " How many centuries, how many thousands of years, have the Kaffir and the Negro held large districts in Africa undisturbed by the white man ? Yet their intertribal struggles have not yet produced a civilisation in the least comparable with the Aryan." Yet he goes on: " History shows me one way, and one way only, in which a high state of civilisation has been produced, namely, the struggle of race with race, and the survival of the physically and mentally fitter race."* If this is so, why does not the savage, whose struggle is the keener, progress more rapidly than the civilised race, where the struggle is mitigated ? †

A just conception of evolution, then, does not support the view that the struggle for existence is the condition of progress. It therefore lends no sanction to the prevailing worship of force. On the contrary, it supplies a broad justification for the ethical conception of progress as consisting essentially in the evolution of mind, that is to say, in the un-

---

* " National Life," p. 19.

† To be just, Professor Pearson seems affected by some consciousness of the contradiction, for he goes on to say : " If you want to know whether the lower races of man can evolve a higher type, I fear the only course is to leave them to fight it out among themselves, and even then the struggle for existence between individual and individual, between tribe and tribe, may not be supported by that physical selection due to a particular climate on which probably so much of the Aryan's success depended " (Ibid.). This is in reality to abandon competition and fall back on the trite pre-evolutionist theory of climate as the cause of progress.

folding of an order of ideas by which life is stimulated and guided. It has been the misfortune of our time that attention has been diverted from this ethical, or if the expression be preferred spiritual, order in which the essentials of progress lie to the biological conditions which affect man only as the human animal. A clearer view of the meaning of evolution should restore the mind to its rightful place, and thus justify the reformers who insisted on the application of ethical principles to political affairs, as against the materialists for whom the ethical consciousness is a bye-product of forces to which in any conflict it must necessarily give precedence.

The application of ethical principles to the social structure, to national and international politics, is merely the effort to carry one step further that guidance of life by rational principles which constitutes, as we have seen, the essence of orthogenic evolution. Religious and ethical teachers aimed first at regenerating the life of the individual, and though often brought involuntarily into conflict with the existing social order, they but seldom set themselves to reconstruct it from the foundation in accordance with their views. The tendency was to accept existing social conditions and show the individual how, taking them as he found them, he could so pick his way among the shoals as to reach his own salvation. But in the modern world this attitude has gradually been abandoned. The pressure of events and its own development impelled the spirit of progress to turn upon social institutions as the immediate and most important object of attack. Collective rather than individual humanity became the supreme object, and accordingly the conditions of social life were found to be the prime means of accelerating or retarding development. Hence the endeavour which came to a head in the eighteenth century to form distinct conceptions of social justice by which the actual constitution of society might be tested. Hence the doctrine that the government should be the servant rather than the lord of the people, which meant that political interests must yield to the common good; that all classes were entitled to equal treatment, which subordinated political privilege to moral justice ; that restraints on liberty should be limited by the demonstrable needs of social welfare, which recognised the moral claim of the human personality to make the utmost of its powers. Amid all differences and conflicts one idea is common to the modern democratic movement, whether it takes the shape of revolution or reform, of Liberalism or Socialism. The political order must conform to the ethical ideal of what is just. The State must be founded on Right—a conception which in the ancient world could only give rise to Utopias, but in the modern period has been the practical cause and canon of many a change. The biological view of evolution opposes this ideal as unscientific and in the end self-defeating. It is for this reason that the biological teaching is so profoundly reactionary and lends itself so handily to the popular cynicism of the day. A truer view of evolution, on the other hand, exhibits the attempt to remodel society by a reasoned conception of social justice as precisely the movement required at the present stage of the growth of mind.

NOTE.—The questions raised in this chapter are more fully discussed in the writer's " Mind in Evolution."

CHAPTER V

SO far we have contended for the conception of Right in opposition to that of
force as the basis of political relations. But
it may be thought that a theory of ethical
evolution which makes the collective progress
of humanity the supreme end of conduct lends
countenance to doctrines of Expediency, which
are no less opposed to those of Right. Let
us then examine the doctrine of Expediency,
or Efficiency as it is now called, in its
modern dress. According to this doctrine it
would seem that good administration is the
sole and sufficient consideration for the
political thinker, while the method by
which good administration is achieved is
a secondary matter. The main thing generally necessary is adequate power for
the expert official. Life seems to be con-

ceived as organised in a number of departments under a hierarchy of officials, each of
whom is an expert in the branch immediately
under his supervision. How the departments
are to be correlated and the supreme experts
controlled is not always so clear. Indeed,
who precisely the expert is, how he is known
and appointed, whether he is qualified by his
own pronouncement to be regarded of all men
as "expert," or owes his position to some
one still more highly qualified than himself;
whether, again (as sometimes seems to be
assumed), the "man on the spot" is always
an expert, or whether it is possible that
inexpert people should sometimes be highly
placed—all these are questions which might
be put to those who throw about the word
so lightly. Sometimes it seems to be thought
that the art of governing men is as mechanical a matter as that of laying drain-pipes,
to be acquired through a similar routine of
instruction and apprenticeship. Having
mastered this routine the expert, it would
almost seem, is qualified to direct society as
its natural governor. At other times the
argument is pitched in a lower key and we

are merely urged to call in the expert for public as we do for private affairs. But at this point it seems to be forgotten that in private life we have at times to keep a somewhat watchful eye upon the experts we employ. Thus the analogy would after all lead us back to responsible government and therewith to all those old principles of popular rights and free discussion which "efficiency" was to supersede. It appears, in short, that upholders of "efficiency" as opposed to principle, and of the expert as opposed to the responsible ruler, have not adequately considered the difference between the specialist and the statesman nor distinguished the functions of determining the end of action and providing the means to the end. But there is a more fundamental criticism. Mechanical organisation is a good thing in itself, and a class of expert officials is an essential element in the working of modern democracy. But perfection of machinery is not life, and may be so used as to destroy life. A government may organise all things well upon its own lines and yet in its very success it may be sapping the strength of its people. On

this point let us take the verdict of no
English Liberal or French idealist, but of
the great German historian for whom Cæsar
represents the highest type of statesman and
the wonderful bureaucratic system founded
by him one of the great achievements of
history.

"The history of Cæsar and of Roman Imperialism,
with all the unsurpassed greatness of the master-worker,
with all the historical necessity of the work, is in truth
a more bitter censure of modern autocracy than could be
written by the hand of man. According to the same law
of nature in virtue of which the smallest organism
infinitely surpasses the most artistic machine, every
constitution, however defective, which gives play to the
free self-determination of a majority of citizens infinitely
surpasses the most brilliant and humane absolutism ;
for the former is capable of development and therefore
living, the latter is what it is and therefore dead." *

What is spontaneous in a people, be it in
the movement of an individual, a class, or a
nation, is always the source of life, the well-
spring of the fresh forces which recruit jaded
civilisation. In proportion as the weight of
government succeeds in crushing this spon-

* Mommsen's "History of Rome," E. T., vol. iv.
p. 466.

taneity, in that proportion, alike whether its administration be conscientious or profligate, aimed at the happiness of the governed or their misery, it tends inevitably to arrest development and inaugurate a period of decay.

It must be understood that much more is at stake here than the wisdom or folly of democracy as a governing body. It is no academic question of the form of government, but the always living question of its spirit, that we are discussing. When administrative efficiency is made the supreme end, personal liberty, and religious and national divergencies become secondary and subordinate matters. There is not much consideration for the weaker brother, nor much patience with the offender. The grinding of the machine wears away these graces of humanity. Even the vestal fire of justice is apt to flicker out in the ideal commonwealth of the efficient. And yet here is another contradiction. For in reality that efficient, upright, expert official on whose actual existence the whole fabric is based is but the product of free government, the creature of close and general criticism, evolved in the environment of a public service in which the feeling of responsibility to the nation has been the slow growth of time and in large measure the special work of reformers who insisted on impartial selection of the best men, and the right of public criticism of every department. Experience has in fact shown that popular government can with due precautions obtain upright and competent expert service. But it has not shown that these qualities would remain unimpaired if the popular element in government were to fall into decay.

Thus the question of responsibility leads us back to the governing rights of the community, and the analysis of progress prevents us from overestimating machinery and compels us to give liberty its due. By both roads we return to the State founded on the conception of Right. This conception must not be misunderstood. There are no absolute or abstract rights of the individual independent of and opposed to the common welfare. Rights are relative to the well-being of society, but the converse proposition is equally true that the well-being of society may be measured by the degree in which their moral rights are secured to its component members.

The mistake of the ordinary doctrine of expediency is to confuse the temporary and the permanent. It would often be to the immediate advantage of Society to ignore some right of an individual or a class. But it may at the same time be for its permanent welfare that the same right should be maintained. For the moral right of an individual is simply a condition of the full development of his personality as a moral being.* Equally the moral right of any community is the condition of the maintenance of its common life, and since that society is best, happiest, and most progressive which enables its

---

* The point of the limitation "as a moral being" is of course that it is not any and every self-development that is good. An education in vice might be regarded as a development of certain faculties of mankind. This is not the place in which to offer an ultimate analysis of the term "moral," but if it is taken as implying "social," development "as a moral being" will mean a development which harmonises with social life, and so fits in with and contributes to the development of others.

members to make the utmost of themselves, there is no necessary conflict between them. The maintenance of rights is the condition of permanent progress. But in the pressing forward of each personality with its claim to make the most of itself—that spontaneous, onward pressure from which progress comes —there is unavoidably a clash of interests, and not necessarily of mere material and selfish interests alone. All living together involves a certain rubbing off of edges, a compromise—a lowering, so to say, of individual demands, and yet human happiness and human progress depend upon many-sided expansion, working out in the free and unimpeded activity of healthful vigour the varied capacities, the divergent lines of thought, the myriad aims and interests in which men seek to realise themselves.

Social order may be achieved through the use of force cheaply and easily by suppressing this individual expansion wherever it is inconvenient. This is simple; but so far as successful it is a complete bar to further progress. As an alternative a higher order may be sought within which individuality has full play, in which law has a moral strength because it is felt to be the guardian of liberty, in which, though no right is made absolute to the prejudice of others, none is ignored in the synthesis achieved. And this is the line of progress. The modern State is higher than that of the Middle Ages or of antiquity because it gives fuller scope to human faculty, because it allows a more thorough liberty while maintaining upon the whole a better order, and the modern State has been founded by the resolute insistence on first one and then another of these rights through which the spontaneous play of human energy obtains a vent. Freedom of conscience, freedom of expression, freedom of worship were the conquests of one age; personal freedom, as against arbitrary government, of another; the right of nationality of a third. It would be difficult to deny that cases may arise in which a government is compelled by necessities of public safety to override one or another of these rights. But it is safe to say that society which is so circumstanced is for the time moving backwards in the scale of civili-

sation. People are fond of insisting that
government should adapt itself to circumstances, but they forget the converse truth
that it should endeavour to avoid being
placed in circumstances which compel it
to action incompatible with its better principles.

The denial by a society of a right which
it has once admitted carries with it its own
retribution. For the nation as for the individual, the automatically working punishment of transgression is the dissolution of
those bonds of duty, those ties of fixed
principle, which are woven with such effort
and loosed with such ease. For the nation
the fatal consequences, if not swifter, are
more certain and more extensive. The
denial of right becomes a precedent, and a
precedent is elastic. Indeed, it may be said
that questions of right run up into questions
of fact, since the question whether a given
right should be recognised by society is
ultimately settled by the question whether
its refusal is in the long run compatible
with the principles on which that society is
based and which it desires to maintain. If

not, no self-deception will prevent the working out of the process whereby the refusal to apply a principle in a given case makes a breach in the ethical constitution of society that can only be made good by repentance and reparation. The effects of successive derelictions of duty on national character are writ large in the history of the contemporary reaction at home and abroad.

But if national wrongdoing is an indulgence for which there is in the end a reckoning, it follows that the most popular of all soporifics for an uneasy political conscience must be abandoned as a quack remedy weakening to the fibre of the system. We are very frequently told that a course of action, being wrong, should never have been entered upon, but having been entered on must, to save our credit, be "seen through." Now in the ethics of force such an argument is intelligible, for in those ethics the first and greatest commandment is, "Achieve your end—if you can, honourably; if not—achieve it." This is consistent. So also is the other rule, "Be just, and so succeed if you may; but if you may not so succeed, be just." What is not consistent is the argument which admits considerations of justice and refuses to apply them. "We ought never to have started, but having started we cannot go back. Our prestige is involved. The first step was foolishness, but the consequences are inevitable." In this familiar strain, what generally strikes us is that at every point the arguments employed to prove the absolute necessity for going a step further are substantially the same, and at each stage there is a party of "moderate men" who tell us that it was great folly to have listened to such arguments before, but a regrettable necessity to accept them now. "Having gone to A, we must go on to B. It is true we ought never to have been at A, but since we are there——." The same argument will take us from B to C and from C to D, or, in fact, as far as the original instigators of the move desire. They at least are consistent; they will gain their ends irrespectively of all other considerations, and from their consistency those who hold by national right may learn a lesson. Those who cry "Inevitable" and "Too late" will always wander creedless in the twilight, but those who take the conception of public justice seriously will maintain that persistence in wrongdoing will not set us right. On the contrary, if we have started on the wrong path, the further we go the worse it will be in the end. We may pile wrong upon wrong to gain our ends, but we shall only pay the more heavily in the breaking up of our traditions, the loss of our self-respect, and the destruction of those things that make a nation happy and great.

To reconcile the rule of right with the principle of the public welfare is the supreme end of social theory. In its early stages modern political philosophy regarded the rights of the individual as prior to the formation of the State. This was common ground to the Tory Hobbes, the Whig Locke, and the revolutionary Rousseau; all alike conceived the individual as clothed with certain rights by nature, and as owing nothing in this respect to the structure of the State, the opinion of his fellow-men, or in short, to the common moral consciousness of mankind. It was precisely here that the contradiction lay, for morally speaking a right can be nothing except what the moral consciousness makes it, nor can it have any effect except in so far as it is recognised by others than the individual who lays claim to it. However, the individual, being conceived by all upholders of the social contract theory to be clothed with certain original rights, was held to part with certain of these rights in order to make a contract with other individuals similarly situated, and form together with them a political society for common defence and mutual help.

The Tory, the Whig, and the Revolutionist naturally differed greatly in their views as to the nature of this contract and the kind of rights which the individual was held to reserve in making it, but the fundamental point of view is common to them all. The rights of man are something absolute and fixed, a remainder that is left out of the original stock of human nature after the deductions necessary for concluding the social contract.

According to this conception, then, the welfare of society must be made to accom-

modate itself to the alleged rights of individuals, and it is easy to see that such a
doctrine would be an appropriate foundation
for a revolutionary movement. To Bentham,
in fact, penetrated by the opposite conception
of social welfare, the whole theory appeared
a mass of "anarchical fallacies." The utilitarian school took up the question from the
opposite end, and laying down the greatest
happiness of the greatest number as the final
end of all action, private or public, and as
the ultimate basis of all rights, saw in the
claims of the individual whether to an
absolute right of property or an absolute
right of freedom, merely so many barriers
to the possibilities of social and political
reform. Each man on this view had only
such rights as society in its pursuit of the
common welfare saw fit to allow him. For
an attack upon vested interests, where the
injury to the common weal was gross and
palpable, no more effective weapon could
have been devised, and the theory contains
an important element of truth. It lays
down the supreme condition of all rights.
It only omits to define precisely how the

generally acknowledged rights follow from that condition, and to decide whether they are to be allowed any secondary or derivative value, or whether they are to be dismissed as the superstitions of an exploded metaphysics. Utilitarianism thus paved the way for the biological theory of society in which, as we have seen, the notion of right gives place altogether to that of force. In the struggle for existence men make claims, but have no rights except the claims that they by their own power can make good. There is no test of desert except success, and no distinction between the good man, the good community, the good religion and the bad man, the bad community, and the bad religion, except that the one drives out and exterminates the other. The rights of man are, in short, the rights of the highwayman. Faced by this conclusion the sociologist is forced to reconsider the whole theory of evolution, and he finds at the outset a distinction which the biologist ignores. The evolution which has created man, which has engendered human society and developed civilisation out of barbarism, is, he finds, not based upon the struggle for existence, but upon an opposed principle by which the struggle for existence is gradually subdued, a principle of peace rather than war, of co-operation rather than competition, of love rather than hate. The progress of this principle is to be traced in the gradual formation of an order of ideas in which, bit by bit, the jarring and conflicting elements which destroy peace are remoulded and recast into a form which admits of their mutual adjustment. The very first formation of a peaceful social order in the barbaric tribe implies the recognition of certain rights and duties, the normal performance of which keeps the tribe together, and as the social order developes both rights and duties are expanded and the conception of them deepened and purified. Every fresh right or duty that men are brought to acknowledge represents one stage further in the development of the ethical order, a fresh perception based on experience of what is necessary for the healthy working of human life and society. From this point of view, though the common morality of mankind does not express final truth, it does express the rough truth which long experience yields.

The true line of rational progress lies not in sweeping away these painfully acquired possessions, but in seeking after an order of ideas in which they can be harmonised and completed. The " rights of man " are partial expressions of ethical truth, which when made absolute clash and conflict with one another, yet a synthesis is possible in which the conflict disappears and each claim is duly regarded. To find this synthesis is always the problem of social ethics. Claims of the individual personality, claims of society, rights of conscience, duties of public responsibility which appear irreconcilable on a lower plane are found capable of uniting on a higher, to the great benefit of the social life as a whole. Hence progress is conceived by the evolutionist as consisting in the working out of a higher order, and in this view he finds a means of reconciling the utilitarian school with the upholders of natural right, for to him, as to the utilitarian, the welfare of society must be the supreme end; but when he looks into

the broad conditions upon which that welfare
depends, he finds it precisely in the maintenance of these rights, which the latter
school hold to be the gift of nature to
man, but which are in reality the late acquisitions of a slow and painful development.
Treating the full development of humanity,
the unfolding of the powers of mind, the
coming to itself of the human spirit, as
the final cause of life, the ultimate aim of
action, and the canon by which right and
wrong are to be judged, the evolutionist
estimates institutions by their bearing on
this supreme end. For him, though no
rights or duties are "natural" in the old
sense, yet some are fundamental—those,
namely, which he finds to be permanent and
necessary conditions of the free, onward
movement of the human spirit.

CHAPTER VI

THE IDEAS OF LIBERALISM

WE have seen that a scientific theory of evolution justifies, as against the creed of force, the fundamental idea of the modern democratic movement — the application of ethical principles to political relations. It remains, however, to ask how the political ideas thus engendered have fared in the light of experience, particularly of our recent British experience. We may begin with the distinctive ideas of Liberalism. These ideas have passed through the ordeal of a reactionary period. Have they come out of it unscathed? Popular sovereignty for instance was an article of the Liberal creed. Put into practice, popular sovereignty has not been very kind to Liberals, nor— which is more to the point for us—has it

THE IDEAS OF LIBERALISM 139

dealt very tenderly with some other Liberal ideas. Is democracy workable under modern conditions ? or is the belief in it one of those shattered illusions with which the period of reaction is strewn ?

Few of those who were formerly convinced democrats would answer the second question with a clear and confident "No." They expected better things of democracy. Many of them were inspired by a belief, which on analysis they would have found it difficult to justify, that the political opinion of the " masses " was morally healthier than that of the " classes," that in getting down to the lower and broader strata of opinion they were also getting to a sounder opinion—an opinion uncorrupted by the " sinister " interests of dynasties, of landlords, or of financiers.

This opinion had at least one ground of support which was no piece of sentimentality. When it was held that the people as a whole have no sinister interests, the meaning was tolerably plain and not easy to confute. A dynasty might govern in its own interest ; a class might govern in its own interest. In either case the interests of those outside the governing body would suffer. But supposing a people, on the same analogy, to govern in its own interests, whose interests would be left out? For thinkers like Bentham, who laid the foundations of English Radicalism, the superiority of popular government to all others followed like the conclusion of a syllogism from the first principles of moral science as conceived by them. Men were in the main guided by self-interest. The unselfish interests, Bentham thought, were well enough for dessert; but the solid meat—the substance on which human life is built, and on which the statesman must rely—was self-interest. But if this were so the only hope for the mass of the people was to give them a voice in the government of their affairs. There was no trusting to the benevolent despotism whether of a monarch or of an aristocracy.

Now, Bentham's philosophical views were too often crude and narrow, but his political deduction has remained, it may be safely said, an integral part of the creed of any popular party. Yet it is a deduction which needs to be very carefully limited and interpreted if it is not to give rise to false conclusions. That the people can have no sinister interests as against themselves seems axiomatic. But, outside mathematics, axioms are too often misleading. Of several criticisms that might be passed on this particular axiom, one will be sufficient for our purpose. Suppose that the completely enfranchised people have to decide on the destiny of another people—a dependency, for example, or a weaker race—then, after all, the logic of self-interest ceases to apply. One nation may act as selfishly, callously, or cruelly in relation to another as one class in relation to another. In the doctrine that the people as a whole can have no sinister interests foreign and colonial relations are left out of account.

To this it would once have been replied that the people have no interest in sub-jugating or fighting others; that the wars of history have been made by dynasties, by churches, by commercial bodies; that these interests have stood to gain by war, while the part of the masses has been merely to suffer and to pay. There is a measure

of truth in these contentions; but the conclusion that democracies would not be warlike—if stated as a universal rule—must
certainly rank among the shattered illusions.
Here again we must distinguish. Few
people are fond of war when the reality
of war comes home to them. But what
those who know war hate most in it is not
the fighting, which appeals to every male
animal, but the attendant circumstances and
consequences of the fighting—the pestilence
and famine, the blackened ruins and starving children. The popular parties of the
Continent are opposed not only to war but
to militarism, because militarism comes home
to them in their own persons and their own
homes. But suppose a population removed
from all prospect of compulsory personal
service, and from all danger of invasion, and
the natural love of fighting will remain,
with no salutary grounds of caution to hold
it in check. Many people in this country
are now under the impression that they
know what war means because they have
seen their friends and relations, young men
of the appropriate age for military service,

go to the front. They do not yet understand that this is only the soft side of war.
It is a different matter when fathers are
torn from their families and business men
from the conduct of affairs, when industry
is paralysed, property wrecked, and the non-
combatant population ruined. This is the
side of war seen by those within the field
of operations. I remember, during the war
in South Africa, hearing of a small trades-
man who said: "I was very keen about
this war. It has cost me ten pounds"—
and he briefly, but with emphasis, reviewed
the incidence of certain duties—"I'll never
shout for another war." This man was
under the impression that he had realised
what war means. Suppose he had seen his
business ruined and his children beggars?
By memory and tradition the continental
democracies have some knowledge of the
realities of war, and it is no matter for
wonder if they are less eager for war than
the English democracy, which has no such
tradition and feels itself secured from all
real danger by the overwhelming strength
of its fleet.

But further, through the prevalence of the
fighting instinct the "interests," as experience has shown, retain their power. They
work the Press and, if they once get the
Executive Government on their side, they
control all the sources of information. Just
as we at home used to get carefully-selected
information from South Africa, less convenient news filtering slowly through when
it was too late to do much harm, so if one
read the South African papers one saw how
equally well chosen items were cabled out
to maintain the required state of opinion
on the other side. With both ends of the
cable in their hands even stupid men can
achieve much. In any international crisis
the experience of years has shown that a
popular agitation is helpless. Its leaders
only know what the Government choose to
let them know. The most damaging fact
—or fiction—can always be produced at the
precise moment when it will hit the agitation hardest, and facts of a different
tendency can be kept back till the crisis
is past. In truth, there is not, and cannot
at present be, any such thing as an effective

popular control of foreign policy. The
average man gives little time and much
less thought to politics. He is a citizen of
a world-wide Empire, the politics of which
consist of an overwhelmingly complex mass
of extremely difficult problems, domestic,
Colonial, and foreign. If he seeks, which he
very rarely does, to arrive at an intelligent
understanding of these problems he is at
once confronted in the Press with a mass
of assertions, true, half-true, or false, of
which, as a rule, none begin at the beginning, but all assume anterior knowledge.
Under such circumstances it may be possible
for him to arrive at an intelligent appreciation of things affecting the interests of his
own locality, or trade, or class; but before
he has had time to educate himself on the
current question of Imperial politics the
crisis will probably have shifted to another
continent.

The old Benthamic principle was too
narrow, but it contains an important truth.
Men are not guided merely or even mainly
by self-interest, but they are guided by the
interests, personal or public, which they

understand and appreciate. Men are intelligent enough and public-spirited enough
to vote down a policy which is palpably
ruining their own neighbourhood. Even in
the most corrupt American cities when the
misgovernment passes the tolerable the
voters rouse themselves and suppress it.
But it is quite different with the ruin of a
remote district of which men know only by
hearsay, which is not constantly obtruding
itself upon them in their daily lives, and
of which, moreover, they hear distracting
and conflicting accounts. The problem of
popular government begins to simplify itself
when it is recollected that no one can
effectively govern affairs that he does not
understand. This has long been recognised
as the limiting principle of absolute
monarchy. The greatest despot cannot
effectively order more than his single brain
can take in, whence the dying complaint
of the autocratic Nicholas that Russia was
governed by ten thousand clerks. Applied
to popular government, the principle shows
us that the greater, the more complex, the
more remote the affairs with which a people

has to deal, the less effective will be its
control. In a vast Empire like ,ours the
popular control of Imperial affairs is little
more than a form, aptly represented by the
appearance of the House of Commons on
Indian Budget nights. It is not so much
that the people manage foreign affairs badly
as that they do not in reality manage them
at all.   For this reason alone Democratic
Imperialism is a contradiction, but it is
possible to admit that and yet to hold that
Democracy without Imperialism is desirable
—that is, to abide by the old principle that
the affairs of any community should be in
the hands of its members as a whole as
against a single family or class. For democracy is government of the people by itself.
Imperialism is government of one people by
another.

But if popular government means, what
the words seem to imply, a form of government in which the mass of the people take
some part, and if the capacity of the people
to take an effective part in government
diminishes as the affairs to be administered
become more vast, complex, and remote,

does it follow that democracy can only be applied with success to small States? Must greater aggregations inevitably tend, under whatever outward form, to the reality of oligarchy or despotism? Some democrats, Rousseau, for example, have thought so. But Rousseau wrote about a democracy that was to be but was not. He had little to go upon except the somewhat misleading experience of the ancient world and the civic republics of Italy and Switzerland. Since his time the world has seen the actual experiment of democracy tried upon the large scale, and the question raised by Rousseau, though not perhaps decisively answered, wears a different shape. To restate it in the form suggested by this experience, we should begin by recognising that democracy means or may mean two things which, though allied in idea, are not necessarily found together in practice. In its most obvious meaning, democracy implies a direct participation of the mass of ordinary citizens in the public life of the commonwealth, an idea most nearly realised, perhaps, in the great assemblies and large popular

juries of Athens. This idea is held by
observers to have materially influenced
American public life, and not to have influenced it for good. It has lent support
to the superstition that the highest and
most difficult of public functions can be
safely entrusted to the ordinary honest and
capable citizen without the need of any
special training as a preliminary. Here is
precisely the point where the contrast of a
small, primitive, simple community with the
vast complexity of a modern nation is of
fatal importance. The village elder, a simple,
well-meaning man, knowing his neighbours,
and familiar with the customs of the country-
side, may doubtless administer patriarchal
justice to the general satisfaction under his
own vine and fig tree, but summon him to the
administration of an elaborate and artificial
system of law and, unless he is a genius,
he must break down. Hence in the teeth
of theory and of the interests of the party
machine Americans are being driven to the
formation of a regular civil service of trained
administrators on the European model.

With the formation of a regular civil

service democracy in its first and most obvious form disappears. There remains the second idea, the idea of ultimate popular sovereignty. In this conception the part played by the individual man becomes less important than the part played by the people as a whole. It is held that the details of government are for the expert to arrange, but the expert administrator holds from the people, receives their mandate, and stands or falls by their satisfaction or dissatisfaction with the result. The people are the ultimate authority, but only the ultimate authority. An immediate power is delegated to politicians who make a business of public affairs, and through them to civil servants with a professional training in administration. It is admitted that the popular judgment can only be formed on the broad results of policy, and must be as much a judgment of persons as of things. It is worth noting that this conception, which comes readily to English writers familiar with our parliamentary system, was also held under a different form by Bismarck, who has explained that not

absolute monarchy, but a monarchy ultimately responsible to, and expressive of,
the popular will, was the ideal always
hovering before him.

Now it may be admitted that the fundamental requirements of democracy are satisfied
if the people as a whole exercise supreme
control over the administration, but it will be
well to ask what are the conditions of this
control. They are, indeed, tolerably familiar,
so familiar that they have perhaps come to be
undervalued. But it must be clear that the
people at large can exercise no sort of control
over affairs, however broad and general, unless,
first of all, they are kept informed, and they
can only be kept informed through publicity
and full freedom of discussion. A few years
ago this would not have seemed worth saying.
To-day it is necessary to say it, and that is
one of the differences that the years of reaction have made. Another thing that would
not have been worth mentioning a few years
ago is that the supremacy of the people is
bound up with the supremacy of law, that
where the executive is above the law the
liberty of the individual and the sovereignty

of the whole body are alike threatened, law being the organ of true liberty. It has sometimes been held that democracy would be no less hostile to personal liberty than other forms of government. It is true, and we have seen it, that the masses may be as antagonistic to personal independence as the classes. A mob may disperse a public meeting as well as the police, and may be an equally effective instrument of the executive Government. But if it is argued that the democratic principle can be hostile to liberty this is a fallacy, for it is full publicity and free discussion that are the organs of democratic government, and if it suppresses them democracy deprives itself of the means of forming a judgment on its own affairs.

Given these conditions, on the one hand the recognised supremacy of the law which it makes, on the other hand perfect freedom to inform itself and make itself heard, democracy, in the sense of ultimate popular sovereignty, is not necessarily incompatible with vastness of territory or complexity of interests. But here there is another point to be noted. With increased size and complexity local differences come into play which threaten, if not to disrupt the democratic State, at least to destroy its democratic character. Within one great State there may be well-marked communities each with a public opinion of its own based on it own traditions, beliefs, and requirements which is no more free to express itself under the government of majorities of a different way of thinking than it would be under the rule of an absolute monarch. Thus Ireland is governed by a democracy, but it is not so easy to say that it is democratically governed. On the contrary, the natural tendency of such a relationship is towards a state of things in which the several conditions of democracy are successively destroyed. In proportion as the subordinate community is strong and determined—in proportion, in fact, as it forms a nation—it will use all the liberty and all the constitutional safeguards which democracy provides as weapons against the dominant majority, and that majority is faced with the dilemma of seeing its power sapped or of contravening the very principles of its own constitution.

From these difficulties democracy has found

a way of escape in one form or another of Federalism. There is the strict Federalism of the United States, with its division of sovereignty and its demarcation of powers between Federal and State Governments. There is also the loose, informal quasi-Federalism of the British Colonial Empire, where in true British fashion lines of demarcation are not too clearly marked, and much is left to tacit understandings, for example the understanding that a Colonial Governor should hold himself aloof from all parties; that all races, at least all white races, were equal in the eyes of the British Government; that the Imperial Government would consult the wishes of colonists in matters primarily concerning themselves. Be this as it may, the development of internal autonomy for each separate part is the means of reconciling democracy with empire, if empire means merely a great aggregation of more than national extent. Five years ago it would have been said that for the British Colonial Empire this reconciliation had been definitely achieved, and that it was not achieved was due to the breakdown of some of those tacit under-

standings to which we have referred. How
far the mischief is irremediable remains
to be seen. Undoubtedly events in South
Africa have added strength to the centrifugal
forces of the Empire—how much may be
measured by the nervous anxiety, which has
become a feature in our politics, to find some
expression of unity which the Colonies will
accept. But this very anxiety tends to
strengthen the forces which it seeks to control,
and the whole position illustrates the extreme
difficulty of reconciling any effective union on
so large a scale with the nationalist aspira-
tions of the component parts.

But whatever its fate in the British Empire,
Federalism has a future, as the natural means
whereby over large areas unity can be reconciled with the conditions of popular government. On the other hand the centralised rule
of dependencies even at its best is inimical to
the democratic spirit. It tends to sacrifice all
higher considerations to efficiency. It regards
free discussion with suspicion. Its ideal is
rather mechanical organisation than the freedom of self-development. These are not the
ideas of national vigour and growth. They

belong to the age of prose, and the age of prose is the first period of the age of decay.   In India the English have doubtless done a great work, and how far or in what sense the idea of self-government is applicable to Oriental peoples is a difficult question on which I do not touch here.   But both in India and in England the very success of Anglo-Indian organisation has had a reaction which is not altogether fortunate.   But whatever may be said of the government of coloured races and the rights and duties involved in the inheritance of such an Empire, there can be no doubt that the destruction of the liberties of white men already accustomed to governing themselves is an act which carries its own punishment for a self-governing people.   Neither the state of war which conquest presupposes, nor the despotic government, military or civil, which conquest brings about, are compatible with vigorous, free political life and growth in the democracy which undertakes them.   They are a violation of its principles, and a violation which reacts on its character.   Democracy may be reconcilable with Empire in the sense of a great aggregation of territories enjoying internal independence while united by some common bond, but it is necessarily hostile to Empire in the sense of a system wherein one community imposes its will on others no less entitled by race, education, and capacity to govern themselves.

It is therefore by no accident that the tradition of popular parties throughout Europe has been to sympathise with the struggle for national independence which makes up so large a part of the history of the nineteenth century. A great part of the inspiration of Liberalism—and without inspiration Liberalism, unlike its opponent, is helpless—has been drawn from the struggle of the nations against Napoleon, of the Eastern Christians against Turkey, of the Poles against Russia, of the Italians against Austria, of the Irish against England. Some modern writers hold that from the democratic point of view all this sympathy with nationalism is mere antiquated sentimentality. It is not, we learn, self-government, but good government that is required. The brains needed to organise good government will be readily found in a great Empire which is to a petty community of peasants as a mammoth store to a village shop. There is a sad want of modernity about these smaller races that struggle to be free. The petty shopkeeper ought to realise that he would be much better off as a salesman at Whiteley's, and similarly the Boer should have reflected how admirably Lord Milner would "organise" him as a part of that great, gold-producing machine, the British Empire. Of national rights this theory makes short work. According to one version there are no such things. There is no right but might—a theory which is in reality the most ancient of all theories, but which reappears periodically in seasons of intellectual dry rot, and always with the same pretension of being brand new and up to date. According to another version, less pretentious and less stale, all "rights" must give way to the well-being of the majority. Now—I have seen this gravely argued—the bigger nation is the majority. Therefore, the smaller nation must yield to it. In the concrete, it is an absurd pretension that thirty thousand Boers have any right to the gold mines that happen to have been found in their territory. All the interests concerned must be taken into account, and are not the interests of fifty millions greater than the interests of thirty thousand ? Some " Socialists " slightly vary this argument. Ideally they admit gold mines should belong not to the British Empire collectively, but to the world at large. But as the world at large has no means of communising them, the task is left to the British Empire, which in turn delegates it to Messrs. Wernher, Beit and Co. —a second best it is true, but what would you ? Anything is better than to leave them in the hands of a Government of peasants, and the type of Socialist in question amuses himself with the belief that he can " organise " the great capitalists for his own purposes. The form of democratic theory which ignores national differences and national rights is the result of a false abstraction. It rests on a mechanical view of society, and lays stress on only one element in the democratic ideal. It treats the State as though it could be formed by any aggregate of men selected at haphazard and endowed with equal voting power. It forgets that patriotism is not a product of the ballot-box but rather a heritage and a tradition, that loyalty is not merely a matter of reciprocal benefit but as much a matter of collective pride, that the law-abiding spirit which accepts the existing order with its constitutionally-voted changes is not the growth of a day, but is deeply rooted in that underlying community of character by which a man is attached even against his will to his kindred and prefers their blunders to the perfect wisdom of an alien. Analyse the difference as you will, and explain it as you may, the State which is also a nation will have a different life from the State which is a fortuitous concourse of atoms, or the mechanical aggregation of a series of conquests. To ignore the difference is to leave a huge sunken rock unmarked on the chart of political prophecy.

On the other side the theory ignores every element in democracy save one. Democracy is not merely the government of a majority. It is rather the government which best expresses the community as a whole, and towards this ideal the power assigned legally to the majority is merely a mechanical means. There are, as has been shown, quite other features of government by no means less essential to the democratic idea, and to these conditions the power of the majority pushed to an extreme may be fatal. It is not a question of the abstract rights of nationality. There are no abstract rights whatever of nationality, or of empire, of liberty, or of property. The rights of an individual are what he may expect from a social organisation based on certain principles, and the test of his rights is this, that their persistent violation is in the end fatal to the principles of the organisation. For instance, the denial of "constitutional liberty" involves the dissolution of democracy. As was shown in the last chapter, every question of right runs up in the end into a question of fact, for the sanction of a right is the penalty which befalls the society that breaks it. If we attempt to lay down a general definition of national rights and apply it—on the old "geometrical method"—with rigid uniformity in all cases, we shall find ourselves speedily involved in a network of contradictory claims, and in the futile effort to escape by means of verbal distinctions that do not correspond

to the real facts of the case. But if we
regard political science as being, like all things
practical, a blending of many considerations,
at the lowest a compromise of different claims,
at the highest a synthesis, we may go on to
ask what weight or value has the claim of
nationality to consideration? Here at any
rate for the democrat the general answer is
much simpler. He is bound to recognise as a
mere matter of fact that where a number of
men are bound together by the peculiar ties of
sentiment which constitute nationality, and
this sentiment does not receive free play from
the government to which they are subject,
then constitutional liberty is threatened, and
if constitutional liberty perishes, all but
the husk of democracy must go with it.
Hence he must admit that the suppression of
a nationality is dangerous to the success of his
principles in proportion on the one hand to the
depth and vitality of the national feeling, on
the other to the length to which the majority
will allow itself to be led in the process of
suppression. He will hardly adopt the current
view that you prove your manliness by sticking
at nothing, not even the total depopulation of

a country, but will hold by the saner principle
that where a nation finds itself being drawn
into courses repugnant to its traditions it is a
sign that it has started on the wrong road.
National rights, then, have their assigned
place in the democratic system, and the
democrat who is told that for his country's
honour or safety she is bound to hold another
nation in bondage, and is asked to assent in the
name of democratic principles and the right
of the majority, must reply that it is only by
dismissing his democratic ideas that he can
do what is asked. He may choose to dismiss
them for the sake of other ends which he holds
more urgent, but he will not, if he is a clear-
headed person, accept the suppression of a
nationality in the belief that he is carrying
out democratic principles.

Nationalism may be exaggerated like everything else, and its most repulsive exaggeration
is precisely Jingoism, whether it takes the
form of mere vulgar aggressiveness or disguises
and deceives itself in the garb of international
philanthropy. But a nation that is merely
standing up for its own rights, and is not
seeking either to conquer or to patronise the

world at large, has always had the sympathy
of liberally-minded men. Nationalism of this
kind has stood for liberty, not only in the
sense that it has resisted tyrannous en-
croachment, but also in the sense that
it has maintained the right of a community to work out its own salvation in its
own way. A nation has an individuality, and
the doctrine that individuality is an element in
well-being is rightly applied to it. The world
advances by the free, vigorous growth of
divergent types, and is stunted when all the
fresh bursting shoots are planed off close to
the heavy, solid stem. Good government is
worth much, but, so far as imposed from
above, more for the life that it makes possible
within it, which will probably sooner or later
conflict with it, than for the material comfort
of which it is the direct cause. Organisation
is worth much, but the most perfect mechanical
organisation is something far inferior to organic
life resting on the spontaneous co-operation of
parts which preserve their independent vitality.

Thus the teaching of our recent history
appears to be not that the older Liberalism is
"played out," but that the several elements of

its doctrine are more vitally connected than appears on the surface. Many people have been inclined to accept popular sovereignty while abandoning the principles of personal and national liberty, of class and race equality. Experience and reflection show that this is impossible. The system of ideas which underlay the older Liberalism was a coherent whole. There cannot be any real popular sovereignty without perfect liberty for the expression of opinion. The safeguards of liberty cannot be maintained when one class or one nationality is being held in bondage by another, even though that other holds power nominally in virtue of a majority of votes. The destruction of liberty again means the moral weakening of law, and the less the moral strength of law the greater the physical strength which government must exercise to enforce it, and the less it can allow question and debate. Thus the forcible government of any section tends to the destruction of liberty for those who govern. Their deliberative assemblies surrender their power, and the end is the enthronement of the bureaucrat in the vacant seat. Whatever else may be said for or against them, then, we may fairly conclude that the ideas of democratic government, personal liberty, the supremacy of law as against arbitrary rule, national rights, the wrongfulness of aggression, racial and class equality are in principle and in practice closely interwoven. They form an ethical whole, and by their application to social and political affairs humanity made the great stride which separates the nineteenth century from the eighteenth. No part of this whole can be abandoned in principle without injury to the remainder, and the attempt to do so has led to the reaction of the last twenty years, by which the winnings of our civilisation are threatened.

CHAPTER VII

THE LIMITATIONS OF DEMOCRACY

IT may be urged that there is a more fatal criticism of democracy than any of those theoretical considerations which we have dealt with. Self-government, it may be said, has in practice broken down. In embracing Imperialism it has, as the phrase goes, "contradicted itself," for the fundamental idea of democracy is not any particular form of government, but the reconciliation of government with liberty, and Imperialism is the negation of liberty. Popular government having thus proved a bruised reed, it is necessary to look elsewhere for social justice, and the conditions of human progress. This conclusion, to which of late many people of popular sympathies have probably felt themselves drawn, is at least premature.

Everything human sins against its own principles, and it is not reasonable to expect that democracy should be exempt from the weaknesses that beset all other institutions and creeds. Our argument has gone to prove that self-government is most liable to break down when a free people tries to make itself lord and master of others. If this is admitted, it is hardly an argument against the principle of self-government, but rather one in favour of carrying out that principle more consistently. It must be allowed that the principle of self-government is at times abandoned by those who ordinarily profess it, but as much could be said of every other principle. The errors of democratic Imperialism are an argument against ascribing supreme wisdom to any self-governing people, but clearly are no argument against leaving people to govern themselves.

Nor is the corruption of opinion and the lowering of the moral standard in public affairs which has so profoundly depressed all thoughtful observers by any means especially imputable to the popular element in our government. Nor is there the smallest reason for thinking that it would be corrected by a government of select Balliol men. The corruption has, in fact, spread from above downwards. All classes alike give way to Jingoism, and shut their ears to reason and humanity ; but the initiative comes from the world of high finance or of high officialdom. In " society " and among the educated middle class the applause is universal. Among the working classes it is less so. The artizans and labourers have failed to check the great interests which are for ever dragging a nation into schemes of aggression. That is a disappointment, but it would be a mistake to attribute to their entry into public life the positive debasement of the moral standard which has coincided with it. There is no reason to think that we should get a better standard from a more restricted suffrage.

Thus, first, it is not democratic self-government but democratic Imperialism that "contradicts itself," and secondly it is not the popular element in our constitution that is primarily responsible for Imperialism. The only illusion that is destroyed is the belief, if it ever was definitely held, that a people enjoying self-government could never be Imperialist. That was, indeed, a hasty belief, for it implied an expectation that self-government would change human nature. The love of ascendency is not peculiar to any one class or race, nor does it arise from any special form of government. All men, as Mill long ago remarked, love power more than liberty. All nations are, with opportunity, more or less aggressive. All are firmly persuaded that in their most inexcusable aggressions they are acting purely on the defensive. All believe that in conquering others they are acting for the good of the conquered; that the only charge that can be laid at their door is that of undue forbearance ; that they are ready to be just and even generous if the others will only submit. All nations believe implicitly in their own entire rectitude and place the worst construction on the motives of others.* All approve of their own civilisation and are inclined to think

* " This dread of being duped by other nations—the notion that foreign heads are more able, though at the same time foreign hearts are less honest than our own, has always been one of our prevailing weaknesses." (Bentham, " Essay on Universal and Perpetual Peace," Works, ii. p. 553.)

meanly of the personal habits of other people. Savage tribes advance upon the enemy with yells; we hurl defiance at them through a certain portion of the Press. The Chinese troops are said to make faces at the enemy with a view to frightening them. This calls to mind a passage of Confucius on which I lighted the other day, and which seems quite apposite at the beginning of the twentieth century A.D. :—

"Yen Yew and Ke Loo had an interview with Confucius, and said, 'Our chief, Ke, is going to commence operations against Chuen-yu.'

"Confucius said, 'K'ew, is it not you who are in fault here?' . . .

"Yen Yew said, 'But at present Chuen-yu is strong and near to Pe; if our chief do not now take it it will hereafter be a sorrow to his descendants.'

"Confucius said, 'K'ew, the superior man hates that declining to say, "I want such and such a thing," and framing explanations for the conduct.'" *

Thus, the Chinese princelets wanted other people's land two thousand five hundred years ago just as European rulers do now. Then, as now, they declined to say so openly; they preferred "framing explanations," and a

* Legge's "Confucian Analects," book 16, chap. 1.

favourite explanation was that unless a policy of " never again " were " seen through," the opposing State, even if at present impotent, might some day be in a position to injure them. In the same conversation Confucius goes on to show, in true Shakespearian spirit, that domestic misgovernment is the true occasion of these foreign adventures. These are matters in which the world changes very little.

"There are instances," wrote Bentham,* "in which ministers have been punished for making peace—there are none where they have been so much as questioned for bringing the nation into war, and if punishment had been ever applied on such an occasion it would be not for the mischief done to the foreign nation but purely for the mischief brought upon their own ; not for the injustice, but purely for the imprudence."

The general conditions of the pseudo-patriotism which consists in hostility to other nations are permanent and universal. The form in which it appears varies in accordance with varying conditions of national life.

We in England, through long immunity, had become wholly ignorant of the nature of the passions raised by war. History does not

* Plan for Universal Peace, "Works," ii. p. 555.

tell us much of these things. It preserves the
glory of war, but suppresses its barbarities and
its meannesses. It says little of that secondary
war of tongues which accompanies the war of
weapons and keeps up the flame of passion.
It preserves the fair exterior of chivalry, and
does not turn its light on the calumnies, the
barbarities, the credulity as of savages which
luxuriate in the national mind in war time.
I remember shortly before the South African
War broke out asking one of the ablest and
most consistent opponents of the policy of
aggression whether he did not think that those
who were then shouting for war would, when
it came, be revolted by its realities. My
friend, who remembered the Crimean War,
took a very different view, and gave me clearly
to understand that from the first moment
of bloodshed it would be all over with argument. This was precisely what Cobden had
found.

" From the moment the first shot is fired, or the first
blow is struck in a dispute, then farewell to all reason
and argument ; you might as well reason with mad dogs
as with men when they have begun to spill each other's
blood in mortal combat. I was so convinced of the fact
during the Crimean War ; I was so convinced of the utter

uselessness of raising one's voice in opposition to war
when it has once begun, that I made up my mind that so
long as I was in political life, should a war again break
out between England and a Great Power, I would never
open my mouth upon the subject from the time the first
gun was fired until the peace was made." *

To go back further than Cobden, here is
Bentham's description of popular patriotism,
and let the reader judge whether it needs to be
modified for use in the present day:—

" The voice of the nation on these subjects can only
be looked for in the newspapers. But on these subjects
the language of all newspapers is uniform : ' It is we
that are always in the right, without a possibility of
being otherwise. Against us other nations have no
rights. If, according to the rules of judging between
individual and individual, we are right—we are right
by the rules of justice : if not, we are right by the laws
of patriotism, which is a virtue more respectable than
justice.' Injustice, oppression, fraud, lying, whatever
acts would be crimes, whatever habits would be vices, if
manifested in the pursuit of individual interests, when
manifested in the pursuit of national interests become
sublimated into virtues. Let any man declare, who has
ever heard or read an English newspaper, whether this
be not the constant tenor of the notions they convey.
Party on this one point makes no difference. However
hostile to one another on all other points, on this they

* Morley's " Life," ii. p. 159.

have never but one voice—they unite with the utmost harmony. Such are the opinions, and to these opinions the facts are accommodated as of course. Who would blush to misrepresent, when misrepresentation is a virtue ? " *

Some of us have been inclined to look back on the time of Cobden as the halcyon days of peace and sobriety and justice between nations. We have been led to think the orgy of barbarism which we have witnessed something wholly peculiar to our time, something that points to a real retrogression towards savagery. There is, in fact, as I have pointed out, a real intellectual reaction. The humanitarianism of Cobden's day is no longer popular. But let us not exaggerate. Human nature has not changed in fifty years. Cobden was a peculiarly able and resourceful apostle of peace, with a peculiarly noble and eloquent brother in arms. He had behind him all the prestige of his great success in the Free Trade movement, and the economic conditions were more favourable to his protest than to that of Mr. Morley and Mr. Courtney. But Cobden had precisely the same forces to fight. There was precisely the same pugnacity, the same

* Works, vol. ii. p. 556.

callousness to outrageous acts done in the British name, the same ferocity of vindictiveness fed by the same agencies. " You must not disguise from yourself," he writes in 1847, " that the evil has its roots in the pugnacious, energetic, self-sufficient, foreigner-despising and pitying character of that noble insular creature John Bull."

Clearly John Bull was no less warlike in the forties than he is now, no less convinced of the necessary justice of his own cause, or of the service which he rendered humanity by condescending to conquer and to rule it. Nor when incidents occurred to throw a very ugly light on those civilising influences of which he was wont to boast was he a whit the more inclined to listen to the truth about himself and his agents. He received the account of the things done in his name with the same callous indifference which is familiar to us. Cobden writes in 1849 precisely as any man of his views might have written on twenty different occasions in the last dozen years :—

" It shocks me to think what fiendish atrocities may be committed by English arms without rousing any conscientious resistance at home, provided they be only far enough off and the victims too feeble to trouble us with their remonstrances or groans." *

Nor is the howl for vengeance anything new. Cobden was terribly impressed by the savagery of the Sepoys in the Mutiny, "but," he adds—

"We seem in danger of forgetting our own Christianity and descending to a level with these monsters who have startled the world with their deeds. It is terrible to see our middle-class journals and speakers calling for the destruction of Delhi and the indiscriminate massacre of prisoners." †

Then, as in our own time, the non-combatants were the most furious for blood. ‡

* "Life," ii. p. 56.

† *Op. cit.*, p. 212. Disraeli in the same connection declared that if such a temper were encouraged, we ought to take down from our altars the image of Christ and raise the statue of Moloch there.

‡ Continuous contact with savages must be reckoned among the causes of deterioration in the practices of war. Generally speaking—though there are interesting exceptions—the savage gives no quarter unless he enslaves his captives, and regards the person and property of the conquered enemy as entirely at his disposal. The civilised man who has gradually put away these methods of warfare in dealing with other civilised men, gradually resumes them when he comes to deal with the savage. Quarter is at times denied, the land and possibly the cattle of a conquered tribe are appropriated. On occa-

In a word, the moral conditions of the controversy were the same in Cobden's day as now. Jingoism and Imperialism were not then known by name, but the same pseudo-

sion they are subjected to forced labour. Even torture, as in the case of the Philippinos, is applied to prisoners. It is inevitable that the demoralisation should spread. The following passage from Hansard for April 17, 1896, is instructive in the light of later events :—

" Mr. Henry Labouchere : I beg to ask the Secretary of State for the Colonies whether his attention has been called to the fact that the villages of the natives of Matabeleland are being burnt by the forces of the Chartered Company, and that a farmer on quitting his homestead left a considerable amount of dynamite, with fuses attached, which exploded when his homestead was filled with natives, killing about one hundred ; whether such proceedings are in accordance with the usages of war, and if not, whether he will take steps to prevent their occurrence.

" Mr. Chamberlain : The burning of the kraals of a native enemy is in accordance with the usages of South African warfare. I have no information of the reported explosion of dynamite in a farmhouse, but if true it does not differ materially from mining operations in a siege or the use of a torpedo in naval warfare."

It will be seen that the burning of farms is here justified as a practice of native warfare. What natives may do the white man apparently may do in fighting with natives, and four years later it is discovered that he may do the same thing in fighting with other white men patriotism which takes the form of hostility to all countries but one's own was there, and was no less powerful. For a number of reasons, economic and political, it took a different form. It was the Palmerstonian ideal of a " spirited foreign policy "—that is to say, of incessant intervention in the affairs of Europe—which Cobden had mainly to combat. And if Cobden was beaten, his ideas in the end prevailed. A generation later it was the extravagant Orientalism of Disraeli, with its correlatives of hostility to Russia and support for Turkey. This in turn was fairly met and overthrown, and Disraeli's first lieutenant admitted his error. Now it is Imperialism, which is at its best a belief in the " civilising mission " of the " Anglo-Saxon " race, and at its worst what we have seen in South Africa, but in essence the same blind, unreasoning, unimaginative, callous, collective self-assertion. What we have to lament is not that something new in essence, and in essence bad, has been hatched out by the devil that is in humanity, but that the real progress that has been made in other things has left us not one whit better—and perhaps, temporarily and in degree, worse—in this relation. This change must be attributed to the coincidence of those intellectual and political causes which since Cobden's time have fostered the growth of materialism—that is to say, the tendency to overvalue physical force and to ignore the subtler and less obvious conditions on which the public welfare rests. But this disease affects the public as a whole, and does not fasten especially on the classes more recently admitted to the suffrage. What is needed is a better public opinion, and this we shall not find by restricting the class to whose judgment we appeal. For improvement we can only trust to the teaching of experience and the re-awakening of those better elements which in our past history have often slumbered but have never died.

On the other hand it is well to be under no illusions about democracy. Free government has not produced general demoralisation, but neither has it, as was hoped, prevented it. The main reason of this failure was pointed out at the beginning of the discussion. In relation to dependencies and weaker races an imperial democracy is a governing class, and it can only be taught as other governing classes have been taught. But there remain certain subsidiary causes of moral failure, partly, it may be, inherent in popular government and partly accentuated by our peculiar constitution. Of these the chief are the dilution of responsibility, and the intermixture of political issues. The individual voter feels but a faint and far-off responsibility for the acts of the Government which he placed in power. His contribution to the result is infinitesimal, and he cannot feel about their conduct as he feels about his own. In point of fact, if any single definite issue of the day be taken as a test the chances are considerable that it is not an issue on which he has been or will be asked to vote. He seldom has to give a definite answer to a definite political question. He is asked a number of questions at once, and asked to say aye or no to them collectively. He votes merely that a certain Government be returned to power, and at the end of a term of years, during which he has no authority over them at all, he can either replace them or turn them out. The attitude of those forming the Government on some questions is known to him, and if he agrees with them on one point while disagreeing on another he must choose between his opinions as best he can. But nothing prevents the men he has put into power from raising quite fresh questions which were not before him at all. If there was at one time an honourable understanding that there was a limit beyond which this could not be done, any such barrier has been swept away in the general overturn. No doubt the voter can in theory punish his Government when their term of power is at an end, but by that time they may have succeeded in raising a new issue, and if the old matter is not wholly forgotten it is subordinated, it may be to some cry of patriotism—it may be to some more absorbing class or sectarian interest.* All that the ordinary voter feels about a given act of government, then, is that it is an act of men to whose return to power he contributed

* The absence of any power outside the Cabinet which, by dissolving Parliament, can compel an appeal from the Cabinet to the nation is the greatest flaw in our constitution, and if not made good will some day lead to serious disaster.

one vote out of some two million or more it may be three or four years ago, when probably quite other questions were under discussion, and whom he will not be able to dislodge until perhaps two or three years more have passed, by which time again other questions have come up. Thus instead of the clear-cut and concentrated responsibility which stimulates and awakens conscience, the responsibility of the voter is as diluted and confused as it well can be. This is one reason why public opinion is often numb and cold to issues of justice and humanity, especially if the right understanding of those issues involves careful study of details and perhaps the sifting of contradictory reports. Men will not be at the pains of such investigation unless they feel their own responsibility to be clear and direct. The work should, of course, be done for them by the Press, but the bulk of the Press will lay before the public nothing that will not be popular. Its business is to tickle its master's vanity, to tell him solemnly that his duty lies there whither his prejudices already lead him, and to cover up and hide away all things done in his name which might be hurtful to his self-esteem. The few who persist in telling the truth share the traditional fate of the honest counsellor at the hands of the mob of courtiers.

Finally, every form of government must be held responsible for the type of man whom it tends to bring to the front, and he who would weigh the merits and defects of democracy must take into account the character of the democratic leader. He must measure the power of brazen self-assertion and unblushing advertisement to bring a man to the front in a society like ours ; he must allow that the capacity of gaining power depends more on the effective use of the rapier or the bludgeon in debate than on any proof of capacity to serve the country, while the art of maintaining power resolves itself into the art of so keeping up appearances as always to maintain the show of success for the moment, trusting to the levity of the public and the shortness of political memories to let the real final reckoning go by without close inquiry. A popular leader is not wont to take long views. He seldom looks farther than the next General Election. It would sometimes seem that he looks no further than the next Parliamentary division, and as long as he keeps his majority, recks little of the effect his words may produce—it may be, on the future of a historic party; it may be, on the broad interests of the nation; it may be, in deepening the wretchedness of some persecuted people in a distant land. If sufficiently endowed with sophistical skill and debating readiness, a democratic ruler may become a very irresponsible being.

It is easier to bemoan the vices of popular government than to suggest a remedy. In part the defects mentioned seem inherent in free institutions—the price we pay for liberty. In part they are fostered and developed by those peculiarities of the public mind in our time to which attention has already been drawn. In part they appear remediable by that simplification of public life which a more consistent carrying out of the principle of self-government would make possible. The devolution of powers, and the shortening of the term of Parliament, would at least mitigate that complication of the issues which at present may almost be said to make it impossible for the ordinary citizen to know what he is voting for, while it plays into the hands of the less scrupulous party leader who knows that he has only to confuse the issue sufficiently in order to escape punishment for his worst misdeeds.

It is natural that the irresponsibility of democracy, and the levity which it permits in its rulers, should lead many people to ask themselves whether a more fundamental reconstruction is not necessary. Free government and the ideals that cluster round it have ceased to charm them, and they would cheerfully barter them in exchange for something more of sobriety, of consistency, of dignity in our public life. Yet the alternative never seems to be clearly thought out. Self-government, with all its defects, implies a recognition of the duties of government and the rights of the people; it postulates a measure of personal freedom and of equal consideration for all classes. It is the natural instrument of a growing sense of social solidarity, and the appropriate organ of a stirring national life. In a word, it is the political expression of the idea of Right on which the modern State rests, and if there be any other mode of government which would maintain that idea equally well, it has yet to be produced.

CHAPTER VIII

INTERNATIONAL RIGHT

WE have argued that the denial of right
is the destruction of democracy. Yet
we were forced from the first to admit that
government being a practical business, dealing
with a thousand diverse considerations and
conflicting claims, can never treat any single
right as absolute. It may be asked whether
these two positions are consistent. The distinction of right and wrong, it may be said, is
absolute, and to admit that a right may not be
absolute is to abandon the ethical view. Let
us consider whether this is so, and let us take
the conception of national right as a test.
Can we, rejecting alike the rule of force, or
bare expediency, and the doctrine of the
abstract rights of peoples, find a concrete principle adaptable to the variation of circum-

stances and yet always and essentially a
principle not of force but of justice? Now it
happens such a principle was laid down for
English Liberals with great clearness and
applied with admirable sincerity over a long
career by the greatest of their leaders. It
is not the special function of a practical
statesman to contribute new germinal ideas
to politics. It is his function rather to
seize and apply the ideas of others, and
in the doctrine of foreign relations which
he preached and practised for fifty years
Mr. Gladstone had predecessors among the
greatest of English statesmen. Yet in his
application of it, the doctrine received so deep
an impress of the personality of the minister
as to seem more his own than any other
man's. It is a striking point in his biography
that the first question upon which he took up
a distinctly Liberal line was one which turned
upon the conception of national duty. The
policy of compelling the Chinese to open their
ports to a baneful traffic repelled him so
strongly as to make him hesitate about joining
Peel's administration. Replying in the debate
of April 8, 1840, to some conventional rhetoric

of Macaulay about the British flag, he asked—

"How comes it to pass that the sight of that flag always raises the spirits of Englishmen? It is because it has always been associated with the cause of justice, with opposition to oppression, with respect for national rights, with honourable commercial enterprise, but . . . if it were never to be hoisted except as it is now hoisted on the coast of China, we should recoil from its sight with horror." *

In the debate on the Don Pacifico affair, he expressed succinctly the principles which determined his conduct of foreign affairs throughout his career :—

"When we are asking for the maintenance of the rights that belong to our fellow-subjects resident in Greece," he said, "let us do as we would be done by— let us pay all respect to a feeble State and to the infancy of free institutions which we should desire and should exact from others towards their authority and strength. . . ."

Again—

"You may call the rule of nations vague and un- trustworthy. I find in it, on the contrary, a great and noble monument of human wisdom, founded on the combined dictates of sound experience, a precious

* Morley, "Life of Gladstone," vol. i. p. 226.

inheritance bequeathed to us by the generations that have gone before us, and a firm foundation on which we must take care to build whatever it may be our part to add to their acquisitions, if indeed we wish to promote the peace and welfare of the world." *

Here we have in essence the ideas upon which Mr. Gladstone founded his foreign policy for fifty years—ideas which have incurred the bitter hostility of a great portion of the public and which seem temporarily to have perished with their first great apostle, but which, as long as Gladstone lived, gave England the reputation of being foremost among nations in the recognition of national justice and in relieving the sorry and perpetual conflicts of national self-interest with some gleams, however intermittent, of a conscience and a sense of humanity.

Mr. Gladstone's principle led him in practise to nearly the same results as those at which the Cobdenites arrived. But it should be noted that his principle is at once simpler and fuller than Cobden's. The Gladstonian theory is not a theory of non-intervention. It is not based purely upon any doctrine of

* *Op. cit.*, p. 370.

individual or of national liberty. On the contrary, it makes room on due occasion for a more positive policy, and by it Mr. Gladstone was led quite logically to intervene in the affairs of foreign nations, and intervene with effect at certain well-chosen moments. The Gladstonian theory is simply that men regarded as the members or as the rulers of a State do not cease to be, either as respects their rights or their duties, the subject of the moral law.* Undoubtedly their rights and duties towards one another are modified by their becoming citizens of the same nation. Englishmen owe certain obligations to one another as Englishmen, which they do not owe as such to Frenchmen or to Germans. They are under obligations to England which they are not under towards France or Germany, but precisely the same holds of any other association

* In outline this theory goes back to Grotius—to say nothing of earlier thinkers—and is the accepted foundation of international law. Gladstone, following a tradition in which names so contrasted as those of Fox and Canning hold conspicuous places, clothed the juristic skeleton with the flesh and blood of a living feeling for righteousness and humanity.

which men may form. The members of a
family owe special duties to one another and
enjoy special rights which each is bound to
respect, but it does not follow that they may
justly ignore the rights of other families.
The father of a family may do for his wife
and children things which he would be held
selfish perhaps if he did for his own sake
alone. So far his rights and his duties are
modified by his position as a member of a
family. He owes duties, again, to his own
children which he does not owe to the
children of another man. But no one would
infer from this that the moral law stops short
at the limits of the family circle. There
remain none the less rights of other families
which each are bound to recognise, and to
disregard which is crime. It is the same
with looser associations based on contract.
A Trade Union calls upon its component
members for a special loyalty, a certain
measure of self-sacrifice, a considerable degree
of mutual support as against others. But no
one would hesitate to censure a Trade Union
leader should he push his own Union to the
point of infringement upon rights of other

associations or of outside individuals. No
society makes such claims upon its members
as a religious body, yet the conscience of the
world has condemned those ecclesiastics who
in the interests of their Church have over-
stepped the ordinary limits of morality. It
is only in the case of the State that some
moral philosophers have attempted to draw
a line and to speak as though right and
wrong stopped at the frontier. But on what
logical ground this distinction between the
State and other human associations is supposed to rest, it is quite impossible to see.
Some writers, starting from the legal rather
than the moral point of view, lay stress upon
the absence in international relations of any
sovereign to enforce the law. They tell us
that in the absence of a sovereign law can
only be said to exist by a kind of fiction, and
that if we are in earnest in desiring to see
law among nations we must look forward to
the formation of a single world State with
a central power to enforce its behests. They
point us to the analogy of the growth of law
in the modern State. In England the rise
of the common law went step by step along

with the extension of the King's peace till it covered all times and all places. It was not, they say, until the kingly power asserted its supremacy over feudal anarchy that law reigned throughout the land. If again we ask how it is that peace has been established in perpetuity between nations which at one time warred unceasingly, like England and Scotland, the answer is virtually the same. It was by the establishment of a common authority. The inference is on the one hand that in the absence of the common sovereign there is no law, and on the other hand that those who desire the reign of law and the permanence of peace should look to the establishment, if possible, of one world empire, or failing that, the consolidation of as many small nations as possible into one or two great empires as the only practical means by which peace can be assured.

This argument, however, rests upon an imperfect reading of history and an inadequate analysis of law. Law does not necessarily imply a sovereign to enforce it. On the contrary, law maintains itself in primitive

communities without the aid of any sovereign or it may be of any courts, yet under
such conditions it is far from being destitute
of force and authority. Rather it is the
expression of custom hallowed by tradition,
backed by supernatural sanction, and enforce-
able when plainly understood by the bulk of
the community. Good authorities hold that
the primitive function of the law court was,
in many instance, not to enforce, but simply
to declare the law, the assumption being that,
a judgment once having been given, the law
was rooted firmly enough in the minds of
the community to enforce itself. Now the
nations of Western Europe resemble a primitive society in two respects. They have no
common sovereign, but they have certain
moral and religious traditions. International
law in point of fact took its rise at the time
when the spiritual power which had conferred
a certain unity on mediæval Europe and
acted, however imperfectly, as an arbiter
between kings, had lost its authority. It was
bitter experience of the evils of international
anarchy that inspired the work of men like
Grotius, and it was the practical need of

recognised rules of conduct that made it possible in the absence of any legislative power to build up a code of international law. The pioneers in the work were wont to appeal to the "Law of Nature" as their authority, but the better opinion of jurists is that it is no ideal code, but the actual custom of nations, on which international rules of conduct are founded, and that the function of international lawyers is to give coherent expression to the best principles which the common moral sense of civilised governments recognises. In other words, international law is like primitive law within the nation, a formal expression of custom resting on the sense of a reciprocal restraint necessary for the common good which is gradually improved as that sense is developed and strengthened. Doubtless the position of the international lawyer would be stronger if he had an international sovereign before whose court he might plead. Yet the problem of forming an international court without a sovereign, and therefore without executive powers, is shown by recent experience to be no more insoluble than was the corresponding problem for primitive society. Few nations could repudiate the distinct finding of an international tribunal, nor in the presence of such a finding have they the temptation to assert themselves, which they have without it, for as long as a dispute is maintained between two rival Powers, the one which yields can always be taunted by foreigners and is certain to be taunted by many of its own journalists with yielding to force rather than to justice, and it is this spurious sense of honour rooted in dishonour which is the standing menace to the world's peace and threatens to make of every trivial incident the occasion for a great war. Nothing is more promising for the future than the manner in which, of late years, nations have shown their willingness to remit secondary disputes to arbitration, and there is every hope that, the precedent being once established, the same principle will be applied to the greater controversies.

However this may be, experience shows a more excellent way towards universal peace than the establishment of a world-sovereignty. Those must have a very poor opinion of the intellects of the friends of peace who bid them seek it by such means. The dream of universal dominion is no new notion. Its realisation has been the object of repeated attempts, the earlier history of which is written in letters of blood and the later history told in accents of disillusionment and despair. The peace advocate who is invited to support such a project may well reply that the wars incidental to the process of conquest are certain, and the prospect of resulting peace dim and visionary. Universal and permanent peace may also be a vision only, but the gradual change whereby war, as a normal state of international relations, has given place to peace as the normal state, is no vision but an actual process of history palpably forwarded in our own day by the development of the international law and morals, and the voluntary arbitration based thereon, which the party of physical force deride.

Even if it be true that law cannot exist without a sovereign to enforce it, the argument would not affect morals. Moral rights and duties are founded on relations between man and man, and therefore applicable to all humanity. To deny this applicability is merely to throw back civilised ethics to the savage state. If there is one thing which differentiates the ethics of primitive man from the ethics of civilised man, it is precisely this. The primitive man recognises duties to the members of his family and to the members of his tribe which are often exacting enough, but to the stranger he recognises no duties excepting in so far as he has entered into certain special relations with him which are guaranteed by supernatural sanctions. Thus, if the stranger within the gates has no host to protect him, he is " rightless." There is no punishment for taking his property or his life ; it is only when he has bound a member of the community to him by ties of hospitality that he can obtain the protection of the law. Similarly the foreign State, unless bound by certain reciprocal obligations, is regarded as an enemy. A common feature of all higher ethical and religious teaching is to repudiate in principle these distinctions, to afford the protection of law and morality to all human beings merely as human beings, and to teach that peace and not war is the normal relation between independent communities. To deny the validity of international ethics in principle is therefore impossible without denying the basis of civilised ethics *in toto*. In our dealings with the foreigner, though we are a State dealing with a State, we are also men dealing with men. If we break our compacts with them we are false, and none the less false because they are foreigners. If we deceive them the lie is no less a lie because uttered in the interests of State. If we bring fire and famine into their land, the suffering which we cause is no less real because felt by men and women of different speech or even different colour. The foreigner bleeds when you prick him just as your compatriot does. Nor is it possible to conceive that we can put off our humanity or any other of the virtues of civilisation in our dealings beyond the frontier, without impairing their sanctity and weakening the force with which they bind us in our dealings with one another. There is no evil power more deadly in public affairs than that of the bad precedent. We cannot deny the validity of a moral prin-

ciple in one relation without sapping its
strength in all.

Critics of the Gladstonian theory raise
puzzles as to the precise delimitation of
national and international rights. They ask
whether every nation is inviolable in its
autonomy, and if so whether we should
repudiate for ever all interference, say, with
the Turkish Empire. They suggest that if
all conquest is immoral, we ought logically to
undo the wrongs of the past. The European,
for example, should cede North America to
the remnants of the Red Indians. They urge
that, if government must be founded on the
free consent of the people, every fragment
of any country that chose to do so could
claim independence, so that if Ireland is
a nation, then Ulster is a nation, and if
Ulster could claim independence so might
Donegal and Antrim. This method of argu-
mentation is merely an instance of the
familiar application of casuistry to ethics.*

* Some of the actual cases of difficulty mentioned,
which have in fact been urged by one of the most
thoughtful opponents of international justice, seem in
reality somewhat trivial. As to the ceding of past con-

It can be applied with equal force against the morals of private life. No moral principle is stronger than the duty of telling the truth. Yet casuists have always been able to puzzle us with ingenious cases in which that duty is

quests, there is even in private law such a thing as the right of prescription. And though the conquest of savage territory has generally been carried out with many circumstances of injustice and barbarity, it does not follow that the occupation of America or Australia by the white man was an injustice in itself. That the owners or occupiers of the soil have an absolute right to it under all circumstances and against all comers, is a principle which may as readily be challenged in the private as in the public sphere. In both cases the right of ownership is met by a countervailing right of access to the means of production, of which we hear too little at home, while we hear too little of the opposite claim abroad. Yet in each case justice, as always, consists in an adjustment of the two claims. To urge the case of the subjects of a tyrant like the Turkish Sultan is a maladroit argument against recognition of the rights of nationalities. There is no question here of interfering with a self-governing nation, but of liberating one race from the tyranny of another.

The problem of minorities, on the other hand, is one of the real and unavoidable perplexities of statesmanship, and appears capable of being solved only by discovering what mode of government is in the special case best reconcilable with liberty, least liable to be driven constantly to special methods of coercion.

overridden by other considerations. There
may be a conflict of rights in national and
international affairs just as there is often a
conflict of duties in private life. Such conflicts necessarily make it harder to lay down
with precision the rule of duty applicable to any particular case. But they do
not affect the principle that the rule, once
ascertained, is binding. On this point,
private and public ethics stand or fall together.

A more serious criticism is to urge that, as
a matter of practical possibility, the code of
private ethics could not be applied in international relations without destruction to the
State which should make the attempt. Private
ethics, for example, carry the duty of self-
sacrifice upon occasion to the point of requiring
a man to lay down his life for another. But
who would teach that such a principle could
be applied to a nation? Apart from this
extreme case, it may be said that the nation
which should endeavour to follow a lofty
standard of duty and honour would, in the
present state of international morality, be in
the position of a man who should carry

Christian principles into effect upon the Stock Exchange, or of a Quaker who should adhere to the strict tenets of his religion in the company of highwaymen. The statement of the argument suggests the reply. Private ethics do not require a man to let himself be led as a sheep to the slaughter. They inculcate rather a quiet and dignified but perfectly resolute maintenance of his own rights combined with scrupulous care not to exceed them, and if any one of the Great Powers were to set itself consistently to maintain such an attitude, it might find its neighbours a little less like highwaymen in their behaviour. Again, private ethics bid a man be prepared on due occasion to yield up his own advantage for the sake of others. But they do not bid him be so yielding as merely to minister to the selfishness of others. So among States there should be a readiness to yield a point for the common good, but none is bound to let others take selfish advantage of its generosity. Further in questions of self-sacrifice, private ethics differentiate between the position of a man who has only to think of himself and of one whose interests are closely bound up with those of other people. Circumstances which would justify me in sacrificing myself would not necessarily justify me in sacrificing my family along with me. Still rarer are the circumstances in which a sacrifice can be reasonably demanded of a nation. Yet material interests are too often sacrificed to prestige, a false form of honour.* They might far more legitimately be sacrificed to some great and enduring interest of humanity. Unfortunately people have not imagination enough to realise that when former Governments have made sacrifices of territorial interests (as in the cession of the Ionian Islands) or of petty pride (as in the Alabama arbitration, or I will venture to add the Pretoria Convention) they have won for their country a higher repute among the nations, a truer prestige as the friend of justice and the protector of the

---

* Thus the present enterprise in Thibet is apparently moving by the accustomed path to the permanent annexation of the country. Many who recognised that this annexation, besides being immoral in itself, will be disastrous to our military position in Asia, yet acquiesced in each step as it was taken, because "prestige" forbade us to retire.

weak, than any aggression of the boldest
buccaneer of our day could achieve.*

There would appear, therefore, to be no
distinction in principle capable of any logical
justification between individual and national
ethics. The State is an association of human
beings—with the exception of the great world
Churches the greatest of all associations. It
has no mystic sanctity or authority rendering
it superior to morality or emancipating it from
the law by which transgression brings its own
retribution in the lowering of character. It
is an association which has its own special
constitution and circumstances, and in the
concrete its duties and rights, like the duties
and rights of every other association and of
every individual, must be judged in relation to
this constitution and to these circumstances.
Such appears to be the full statement of the
Gladstonian principle of internationalism—

* It is one of the paradoxes of patriotism that any
act of a British Government in which concessions are
made from motives of generosity or justice is habitually
attributed in the Press and on the platform to the basest
motives of pusillanimity. Thus consciously to travesty
the noblest actions of one's country is common form to
the popular patriot.

the greatest contribution of its author to political thought and practical statesmanship, in which the long development whereby civilised ethics have emerged from barbarism is completed, and the obligations of patriotism are reconciled with the sovereign duty to a common humanity.

CHAPTER IX

PERSONAL freedom, Colonial self-government, national rights, international peace, Free Trade, reduced expenditure—these were the watchwords of the old Liberalism. To many of us a few years ago they seemed worn-out phrases which would never again kindle fire. Some of them, indeed, we found not seldom used for obstructive purposes, urged in bar of many a plea for measures of social reform denounced in their name as socialistic. We began to hear them with a certain impatience. The old Liberalism, we thought, had done its work. It had been all very well in its time, but political democracy and the rest were now well-established facts. What was needed was to build a social democracy on the basis so prepared, and for that we needed new formulas, new inspirations. The old individualism was standing in our way and we were for cutting it down. It was this mood, as remarked in Chapter I., that disposed many people favourably towards Imperialism as a " positive " theory of the State in external relations parallel to that positive theory in domestic affairs which they demanded for their cherished plans of social and industrial reform. In this mood many men of strong popular sympathies were for kicking down the ladder by which they had climbed to the point of vantage from which their social reforms became possible. But apart from the question of gratitude, to which men allow no place in politics, it is well for a man to be sure that he has his feet firmly on the top of the wall before he kicks the ladder aside. That the work of the old Liberalism was done once and for all was a too hasty assumption. For in part it was a struggle with institutions which, like the House of Lords, still retain their vitality ; in part it was a fight with vested interests, which, though they have changed their character and their methods, are as strong as ever ; and in part it was a crusade against weaknesses and follies of the natural man, in which final victory is never won, but success is to be measured only by the determination with which the war is waged.

The unfolding of the true meaning of Imperialism gradually, as we have seen, rallied men round the old standard, and it is one of the paradoxes of the reaction that the doctrines of the old Liberalism have found some of their staunchest defenders among men who had been wont to look upon most of those doctrines as at best worn-out platitudes and at worst texts useful for the obstruction of further progress. The fight made by the Labour party and the Socialists generally against the South African War will not readily be forgotten, and here, as in the defence of Free Trade, the Socialist leaders and the most notable spiritual descendants of Cobden and Mill stood upon the same platform. Was this alliance an accident, or did it arise out of the nature of things, the logical working out of principles in political practice ? We touch here an important question of principle, which we shall best approach by reverting for a moment to the attitude of the older Liberals towards domestic reform.

Among the older Liberals Cobden's name stands as the type of irreconcilable opposition to everything tainted with a socialistic tendency. Yet we have seen that even in Cobden's case there were qualifications which are too often left out of sight. We have seen that he favoured free education and the prohibition of the employment of children under thirteen in factories. It remains true that Cobden was opposed to the regulation of adult male labour whether by Trade Unions or by legislation, and here there is a real divergence between his view and that which animates " socialistic " legislation. Let us try to be clear as to the ground of the divergence.

Cobden held by freedom of contract on the ground that as a rule the adult sane man is the best judge of his own interests, and that when each party to the bargain is free to take it or leave it, the bare fact that it is concluded is sufficient evidence that it is for the advantage of both. It is in strictness implied in this argument that if the conditions do not hold, the

principle of non-intervention does not apply.
If either party to a contract is not perfectly
free to choose or reject, if he has not full
knowledge of the circumstances, if he is not
capable of forming a judgment, if he is so
circumstanced that refusal is not really within
his option, or is within his option only on pain
of incurring penalties much heavier than those
which would fall on the other party, then the
contract is no longer free and equal. As we
have seen, in the case of children, Cobden
himself insisted that the conditions of true
freedom did not apply. The factory child was
not free to decide whether or not it would
work eight, ten, or twelve hours in a cotton
mill. The decision was made by its parents;
but even if the child were free to decide, it
would not be a competent judge of its best
interests, and even if it were a competent
judge of its best interests, it would not be in a
position to bargain upon equal terms with its
employer. At this point, therefore, Cobden
was in favour of the State stepping in and
deciding for the child and for its parents that
the long hours at work in a factory were bad
for it, and were not to be permitted, and in so

doing the State had this further justification, that even if hardships were inflicted upon some individuals by the prohibition, the community as a whole could not tolerate a form of labour calculated to undermine the health of the rising generation. That is to say, in prohibiting the labour of children two principles were recognised which carry us a long way. On the one hand it was admitted that apparent freedom of contract was not necessarily real freedom; on the other hand it was insisted that the State has an interest in, and a responsibility for conditions, which, operating upon a large scale, determine the health and welfare of its own members. But these two principles, admitted in a leading concrete case by Cobden, are precisely the principles on which the advocates of much of what is called "socialistic" legislation habitually rely. That legislation falls into two main departments. On the one hand, it is directed to the redressing of inequality in bargaining. This was the avowed object, for example, of Irish land legislation. The position taken up by Mr. Gladstone and all who have followed in his footsteps was that it is a mere pretence to talk of a fair and open bargain between the Irish landlord and the cottier tenant. To say that the cottier was free to take or leave the offer made to him was in a verbal sense accurate, but in relation to realities, profoundly untrue. The tenant had in reality no other option. The starving man is nominally free to take or reject the last loaf of bread, but in reality he acts under constraint, and if the baker extorts from him a fabulous price, he avails himself, not of the freedom, but of the necessities of his customer. Now, the principle adopted by Mr. Gladstone was that where the necessities of one party deprived the apparent freedom of choice of all reality, it is legitimate for the community as a whole to step in and regulate the bargain. But if we look at the matter a little more closely, the actual freedom of choice is in all contracts a variable quantity. The two parties are seldom on equal terms, and here freedom and equality are, as often, correlative. As soon as A's necessities are greater than B's, A ceases to stand upon an equal footing; he ceases to be perfectly free to accept or reject B's offer, and B gets the better of the bargain. In the ordinary transactions of commerce these inequalities tend to equate themselves, the advantage being one day on A's side and another day on B's; but where a whole class of men is permanently at a disadvantage in its bargains with another, for example, where one class is economically weaker, by the strict Gladstonian principle the State has a right to intervene as arbitrator, provided that it can do so with sufficient equipment of knowledge and impartiality.

This right it has exercised in a long series of Factory and Workshops Acts, Mines Acts, Workmen's Compensation Acts, Truck Acts and the like, limiting hours of work, restricting the labour of women and children, prescribing for the safety and health of operatives, prohibiting or limiting payments in kind, ensuring compensation in case of accidents. In all these cases freedom of contract is in a sense over-ruled. A workman may be willing to disregard certain risks, but the law forbids it. A woman may be anxious to work longer hours and increase her small wage, but the law forbids it. Often a special clause specifically forbids "contracting out" of the benefits of an Act. These restrictions are imposed in the belief that, if unprotected by law, the operative is often constrained by the pressure of immediate necessity to accept work under conditions injurious to himself or to his family. He is not free in making his bargain because he is not equal to the other party, and the object of the law is to obtain for him conditions on which, if he were free and equal, he would, it is held, insist.

Rightly understood, therefore, this kind of socialistic legislation appears not as an infringement of the two distinctive ideals of the older Liberalism, "Liberty and Equality." It appears rather as a necessary means to their fulfilment. It comes not to destroy but to fulfil. Similar reasoning explains the changed attitude of Liberals to trade unionism. Cobden, as we know, was impressed with the dangers of trade unionism rather than with the benefits which it promised to the working classes. It must be admitted that trade unionism involves coercion and is, so far, opposed to the liberty of the individual in certain relations, but experience and reflection have convinced most men of popular sympathies that the liberty which trade unionism sacrifices is less important than the liberty which it gains. For here again the justification lies in the economic inequality between the workman and employer, inequality which results in unfreedom. Before the law, workman and employer may be in every respect free and equal, but in so far as the one is normally hampered by the overwhelming pressure of immediate needs, while the other, if he loses one workman, can find another, and is threatened at worst with the loss, not of his subsistence, but of a fraction of profit, the bargain between them is not a bargain between equals nor a bargain which both alike are free to take or leave. To redress the balance, workmen have combined, since by acting in concert they can put upon the employer a constraint equal to that which he can bring to bear upon them. In some instances they have succeeded so well that the balance of power is on the other side, and no doubt there have been occasions on which, like all other people who have newly come into power, they have used their power unwisely. That is to say, they have interfered with the liberty of employers or workmen in a manner which the interests of the larger liberty do not necessitate. Precisely how far they can be justly charged with these failings I need not here inquire. For our present purposes it is enough that the broad principle of trade unionism is justified, not as over-riding, but as conserving and promoting liberty and equality in the relations between employers and employed.

So far, then, it appears that what seem on the surface to be the main departures from the principles of liberty and equality, which have commanded the approval of the average modern Liberal, are in reality departures by which the principles of liberty and equality are developed and extended. It results that the breach of principle between the Liberalism of Cobden's time and the Liberalism of to-day is much smaller than appears upon the surface. If we consider a second line of objection to what used to be called State interference, we are brought to a very similar result. A considerable part of the dread of Governmental action felt by the men of Cobden's

day was due to the habit of looking upon
the Government as an alien power, intruding
itself from without upon the lives of the
governed. We, on the contrary, habituated
by the experience of a generation to looking
upon the Government as the organ of the
governed, begin to find even the phrases of
Cobden's time unfamiliar and inexact expressions of the facts. Here fundamentally the
difference is rather in the facts themselves
than in our attitude to them. In Cobden's
day the Government was the organ of the
aristocracy, tempered by middle-class influence. In our own time it is, very imperfectly,
the organ of the community as a whole, and
the conception of popular sovereignty—the
principle that the Government should carry
out the popular will and be responsible to the
people for the manner of its action—would
not be openly denied by any party. Before
popular government was established the
leaders of democratic thought were men
opposed by their very position to the powers
that were. They were in permanent opposition, their work was associated with criticism
of Government; they were concerned to point

out how much it did ill, and it was not their
part to insist upon the occasions upon which
it did well. Like all controversialists, they
were tempted to generalise their arguments,
and to justify their opposition to the Government with which they had to contend by
principles limiting the action of all Governments, however constituted. In this way the
doctrine of popular liberty, which enshrined a
social truth of permanent value, became
identified with doctrines restricting collective
action, which were of merely temporary value.
The change which has taken place in the
minds of popular statesmen since Cobden's
day is due to the realisation of the democratic
principles for which the men of Cobden's time
fought. When the people had once applied
the saying of the French King to themselves,
and declared with truth, " The State, it is
we," when they could look upon the Government as their servant and the acts of the
Government as their acts, it followed necessarily that the antagonism between democracy
and governmental action fell to the ground.
In its place there arises a stronger sense of
collective responsibility and a keener desire

for the use of the collective resources and organised powers of the community for public needs.

Cobden and Bright insisted, none more forcibly, on the moral responsibility of nations, but for the reasons stated this moral responsibility naturally took with it a negative colour. They were far more afraid of what the State would do than of what it would neglect. But the habit of thinking produced under a vigorous democratic polity necessarily gives a more positive character to the conception. A community which governs its own affairs and is master of its own resources is under obligation to provide for its members and for future generations, and, where it fails to do so, is open to the charge of neglect. Here we have the line of thought which justifies State Education, Poor Law, sanitation, and all the improvements of town life for which the present generation have to thank the advanced school of municipal reformers. The mention of education, which Cobden held fifty years ago should be perfectly free, is again sufficient to show that the breach of continuity is no fathomless gulf, but, once more, the responsibility which Cobden admitted in special cases has, under changed conditions, been generalised and adopted as a principle.

If from Cobden we turn to the plea for liberty as stated in an argument of imperishable value by Mill, we shall be confirmed in the view that " Socialistic Legislation " is no destroyer of the old covenant. Mill, who treats liberty in a wider sense of emancipation, not merely from law, but from the pressure of opinion and custom, has three main pleas to urge on its behalf. The first of these is the fallibility of mankind; majorities may be wrong just as Governments may be wrong, for new truth is in a minority of one when first thought of, and it has to struggle often through oppression and obloquy to make its way. What holds of truth holds also of valuable customs, and the sum and substance of Mill's argument is that to meet by force that which should be met only by argument and persuasion is to put humanity in permanent danger of losing sources of enlightenment and progress. Mill's second plea is that individuality is a positive element in well-being. It is better that men should differ than that they should all be cast in one mould. It is better that each should lead his own life, developing his faculties in his own way, and make the most of himself by his own efforts, than that all should be drilled into a mechanical perfection.* All that Mill has to say on this point is a commentary on the Aristotelian view, that to unify overmuch is not good. Lastly, and in close connection with both of the above points, Mill pleads for character and conviction as against a dull assent and a slavish subservience. These are principles of permanent value. It is hardly too much to say that they underlie the whole structure of

---

* It should be noted that Mill's argument cuts deeper than that of Green (his true successor in the line of political thinkers). Green conceives liberty as the right of a man to make the best of himself—a noble conception, but one that does not meet the vital question, whether a man is to judge for himself what is best for himself. Mill's argument implies that a man has the right to make his own mistakes, or, to put it more fully, that that society is best ordered and contains within it the most seeds of progress which allows men most scope to gain their own education from their own experience.

the modern State and sum up that which differentiates it from older and lower forms of political society, but it is clear that they in no way run counter to the principles laid down above as the ground thoughts of modern social legislation.

It is therefore not so very surprising that Mill—one of those rare minds capable of life-long growth—gravitated in later life towards opinions which in his own words would class him and his friends "decidedly under the general designation of Socialists." Mill's statement of the socialistic ideal remains one of the best attainable :—

" While we repudiated with the greatest energy that tyranny of society over the individual which most socialistic systems are supposed to involve, we yet looked forward to a time when society will no longer be divided into the idle and the industrious ; when the rule that they who do not work shall not eat will be applied not to paupers only, but impartially to all ; when the division of the produce of labour, instead of depending, as in so great a degree it now does, on the accident of birth, will be made by concert on an acknowledged principle of justice; and when it will no longer either be, or be thought to be, impossible for human beings to exert themselves strenuously in procuring benefits which are not to be exclusively

16

their own, but to be shared with the society they belong to. The social problem of the future we considered to be, how to unite the greatest individual liberty of action with a common ownership in the raw material of the globe, and an equal participation of all in the benefits of combined labour.

.   .   .   .   .

"Education, habit, and the cultivation of the sentiments will make a common man dig or weave for his country as readily as fight for his country." *

The Liberal and the Socialist have attacked the problem of progress, or what is the same thing, of social justice, at different sides. The Liberal stands for emancipation and is the inheritor of a long tradition of men who have fought for liberty, who have found law or government or society crushing human development, repressing originality, searing conscience. Against this repression the Liberal is for the unimpeded development of human faculty as the mainspring of progress. The Socialist, or if the vaguer term be preferred, the Collectivist, is for the solidarity of society. He emphasises mutual responsibility, the duty of the strong to the weak. His watchwords are co-operation and organisa-

* " Autobiography," p. 232.

tion. The two ideals as ideals are not
conflicting, but complementary. For after
all it is not every development of every
faculty that can reasonably be desired for
the sake of progress. There are mischievous
as well as benevolent talents capable of
cultivation, and if we are asked for a test
to distinguish the two, we can give none
more simple than that of the capacity of
harmonious working in an ordered society.

Both creeds are readily perverted, and it is
then natural that they should conflict. The
principle of liberty may be converted into an
unlovely gospel of commercial competition,
in which mutual help is decried as a means
of saving the feckless and inefficient from the
consequences of their character, the impulses
of pity and benevolence are repressed, and
the promptings of self-interest invested with
the sanctity of a stern duty. Merit is
measured by success, and the standard of
success is the money-making capacity.
Collectivism is liable to a corresponding
distortion, which appears in particular to
have befallen certain forms of Socialism in
England. The Liberal and democratic

elements are gradually shed, and all the interest is concentrated on the machinery by which life is to be organised. Everything is to fall into the hands of an " expert," who will sit in an office and direct the course of the world, prescribing to men and women precisely how they are to be virtuous and happy. We have seen above that there are some difficulties about the character of the expert. In the socialistic presentment he sometimes looks strangely like the powers that be—in education, for instance, a clergyman under a new title, in business that very captain of industry who at the outset was the Socialist's chief enemy. Be that as it may, as the " expert " comes to the front, and " efficiency " becomes the watchword of administration, all that was human in Socialism vanishes out of it. Its tenderness for the losers in the race, its protests against class tyranny, its revolt against commercial materialism, all the sources of the inspiration under which Socialist leaders have faced poverty and prison are gone like a dream, and instead of them we have the conception of society as a perfect piece of machinery pulled by wires radiating from a single centre, and all men and women are either "experts" or puppets. Humanity, Liberty, Justice are expunged from the banner, and the single word Efficiency replaces them. Those who cannot take their places in the machine are human refuse, and in the working of a machine there is only one test—whether it runs smoothly or otherwise. What quality of stuff it turns out is another matter. A harder, more unsympathetic, more mechanical conception of society has seldom been devised.

Now these distortions of Liberalism and Socialism are in necessary conflict. But the true Socialism is avowedly based on the political victories which Liberalism won, and as I have tried to show, serves to complete rather than to destroy the leading Liberal ideals. I may be told that I have ignored the fundamental point that Socialism is an attack on property which Liberalism would preserve. It is, I think, truer to say that the Collectivist's conception of property follows logically from his analysis of the State, and is in accord with the view to which the best political thinkers seem to be tending. Property is not an absolute right of the individual owner which the State is bound to maintain at his behest. On the contrary, the State on its side is justified in examining the rights which he may claim, and to criticise them, seeing that it is by the force of the State and at its expense that all such rights are maintained. Further, it is under shelter of the State and its laws that men accumulate wealth, and the precise nature of those laws has a good deal to do with the methods by which wealth may be accumulated. Now there are some ways of accumulating wealth which depend merely on the growth of society—the increment of land values in towns is an important case in point. Another road to wealth lies through monopolies and privileges granted by the State, exemplified on the one hand by licences to sell liquor, on the other by the common municipal monopolies of the gas and water supply, the tramcar service, &c. The Collectivist holds that all these sources of wealth are in a special sense created by society, and should be retained as far as possible in the

hands of society to meet those collective
responsibilities of which we have spoken.
But how many Liberals are at issue with him
here? The Collectivist, however, would carry
his analysis of property a step further. He
would urge that the main justification of
private property is that he who works should
be able to rely on obtaining an equitable
proportion of the fruits of labour performed
for the common good, and he could show
good reason for thinking that some such
principle, operating perhaps unconsciously,
did in reality split up the old communal
tenure of land—in which the bad cultivation
of one holder would greatly impair the better
work of another—and so led to private ownership. Now, looking at modern industry, he
would think it fair to ask how far this
principle is secured, and he would find certain
great sources of private wealth to which it
does not apply. By inheritance, for example,
a man may acquire wealth without work. By
speculation, again, he may make a great fortune, and though speculation no doubt involves
the exercise of great powers of brain it can
hardly by any stretch of optimistic charity be

looked upon as labour service done for the common good. Aggregations of wealth not acquired by labour service are, I apprehend, regarded by the Collectivist as a kind of surplus from which the funds necessary to meet public responsibilities should in the first instance be drawn. With the laws of inheritance society has in fact always dealt as it has seen fit, and has more than once altered them fundamentally in the course of history. In marking out inherited property as an appropriate source of revenue, the Collectivist is again in full sympathy with the principles of the last great Liberal Budget, and has no revolution to propose. If a method could be devised for similarly taxing the profits of speculation, it would, I have little doubt, command the full sympathies both of Collectivists and of Liberals. But the Collectivist would look forward to the gradual extension on the one hand of municipal and national ownership of certain sources of wealth, and on the other of voluntary co-operation on the federal principle by which the opportunities of the speculator would be gradually curtailed.

Here again the Collectivist, particularly on the burning question of municipal government, usually has the complete sympathy of the Liberal. The reaction, on the contrary, is fiercely contending for the old system of private monopolies as against municipal control.

This seems to be the real character of the "attack on property" to be apprehended from any rational Collectivism, and in support of the view taken, I will venture to transcribe the main heads of the programme officially adopted in 1891 by the German Social Democrats. The German Socialists have the character of laying more stress on the ideal, and less on practical expediency, than we do in England, so that if we do not find their practical programme very remote from those of the ordinary English Liberal, we need hardly fear that a worse thing will befall us in our own practical land. Now, the prelude to the programme undoubtedly sets forth among other things, that :—

"The conversion of the capitalistic private property in the means of production—land, mines, raw material, tools, machines, means of communication—into social property, and the transformation of the production of wages into socialistic production, carried on for and through society,"

are necessary for the welfare of the workers.

This is a wide and far-reaching principle. It may fairly be called a revolutionary principle. But it is so wide and far-reaching that its real meaning is hardly intelligible apart from the practical measures in which it is to be embodied. What, then, are the actual measures which the Social Democrats would initiate if they came into power.

"Proceeding from these principles, the Social Democratic party of Germany now demands:—

1. "Universal, equal, and direct suffrage with vote by ballot for all men and women of the Empire over twenty years of age."

(Other constitutional reforms follow.)

2. "Direct legislation through the people, by means of the right of proposal and rejection."

(Local self-government and election of officials are added)

3. "Training in universal military duty . . . Settlement of all international differences by arbitration."

4. "Abolition of all laws which restrict or suppress the free expression of opinion, and the right of union and meeting."

5. "Abolition of all laws which, in public or private matters, place women at a disadvantage as compared with men."

6. " Religion declared to be a private matter. No public funds to be applied to ecclesiastical and religious purposes."

7. " Secularisation of the schools. Obligatory attendance at the public people's schools."

(With further provisions for free education.)

8. " Administration of justice and legal advice to be free."

(Elective judges, criminal appeal, abolition of death penalty, &c.)

9. " Medical treatment, including midwifery and the means of healing, to be free. Free burial."

10. " Progressive Income and Property Taxes," graduated succession duty; " Abolition of all indirect taxes, customs, and other financial measures which sacrifice the collective interest to the interest of a privileged minority."

There follow demands for—

(1) " National and international protective legislation for workmen " on the following basis :—

(a) An eight-hour day.

(b) " Prohibition of money-making labour of children under fourteen years."

(c) " Prohibition of night-work, *exceptis excipiendis*."

(d) " Thirty-six hours' unbroken rest in every week."

(e) " Prohibition of the truck system."

2. " Supervision of all industrial establishments . . . by an Imperial labour department."

3. " Agricultural labourers and servants to be placed on the same footing as industrial workers; abolition of servants' regulations."

4. " The right of combination to be placed on a sure footing."

5. " Undertaking of the entire working-men's insurance by the Empire, with effective co-operation of the workmen in its administration." *

The candid Liberal, imbued with the current conception of Socialism, will, I think, observe with surprise that out of the first ten heads, seven are expressions of views not perhaps held by all Liberals, but certainly as closely associated with the older generation of Liberals as with those supposed to be tainted with Socialism.

The next two contain proposals which may, or may not, be practicable, but certainly imply no revolutionary attack on property. The tenth consists partly of proposals realised in the Budget of 1894, partly of ideas shared by many English Liberals as possibilities for a future Budget, and partly of a defence of Free Trade. There follow five heads of proposals for industrial legisla-

* I have taken the above from Mr. Thomas Kirkup's " History of Socialism "—a judicious account in which the better meaning of Socialism is sifted out from its extravagances, with the kind of sympathetic criticism so eminently needed, and so rare.

tion, which are all on the lines familiar to us in this country.*

I venture to conclude that the differences between a true, consistent, public-spirited Liberalism and a rational Collectivism ought, with a genuine effort at mutual understanding, to disappear. The two parties are called on to make common cause against the growing power of wealth, which, by its control of the Press, and of the means of political organisation, is more and more a menace to the healthy working of popular government. There is in this country at present no sign of the kind of class war to which German Socialists appealed. There is, we may hope, too general a feeling for the common weal, and there is certainly too intricate an intermingling of classes. Our industrial system does not as a fact tend to that sharp separation of the proletariats from the captains of industry, on which the

---

* It is doubtless true that these are only the immediate demands of the party, but the point is that what lies beyond is vague, and so much of Socialism as takes practical shape turns out to be in the natural line of Liberal progress.

Marxian teaching was based. Our danger is rather that through the development of joint-stock enterprise, the masters of wealth may acquire an ever-extending clientèle, who will prefer their sectional interests to the common weal. Having a great party, and one branch of the Legislature wholly in their hands, they are readily able to frustrate reforming legislation, and to preserve and increase the privileges of great interests to the prejudice of the public. They have had in their favour the exaggerated dread of Socialism diffused among the middle class; though the burden of taxation which they have imposed probably exceeds that which the most far-reaching schemes of social reform would have rendered necessary in the same period. They have thus been able, not merely to keep reform at bay, but in many directions to undo the work of past generations.

Yet there is a limit to their power. As the great interests play into each other's hands, first one principle and then another is violated, which all who think for the common wealth hold dear. At one moment it is our good name for national fair dealing that is smirched; at another it is the principle of religious equality that is infringed; at another it is Free Trade which is menaced; at another freedom of combination.   Such successive onslaughts cause searchings of heart, and shake the sense of security in the enjoyment, without effort, of the good things which past reformers won with the sweat of their brow—that fatal temper of easy optimism which prepared the way for reaction.   Roused from this mood, even those who hesitated about further progress begin to see that the question is rather how much of the ground already won is to be held.   They have learnt that in public affairs there is a current which sweeps us backward when we think to rest upon our oars.   They begin to understand that, in presence of a general and far-reaching reaction, threatening as it does the whole basis of the political freedom, so painfully achieved, it is time to sink minor divergencies of interest and predilection, and learn, even from opponents, the secret of united action.

To sum up in the fewest possible words the main points of the discussion, we have found that the causes of the reaction may be classed under two main heads. As in all far-reaching movements of opinion, sociological and moral or intellectual factors have been at work together. Sociologically, we find the cause of reaction in the growing concentration of material interests. The power of wealth has increased, and the different interests, for which wealth is a higher consideration than life, have learnt the secret of co-operation. On the moral or intellectual side, we have found that the humanitarian philosophy of a past generation has given place to various schools of thought, which from different points of view have tended to discredit the conception of right, and in one form or another to justify the sway of expediency, or even of brute force. Thus the dominant social forces find for themselves that justification which they need in the prevalent popular philosophy. Yet, when we look again into the old humanitarian ideals and ask how they fare in the light of the reaction which has temporarily de-

throned them, we do not find their moral
force impaired.   On the contrary, we are
enabled by a partial experience to judge
better how much we should lose by dis-
carding them for ever.   We have seen that
these ideals are popularly regarded as having
been exploded by evolutionary science, but
we have seen also upon deeper examination
that that theory of evolution which was
supposed to undermine them proves to be
their most effective philosophical support.
The humanitarian ideal is no mere sentimentality, which a just conception of the forces
which mould society is bound to destroy.
On the contrary, it is the legitimate product,
and the highest product, of healthy evolutionary growth.   A truer, because more
complete, science of evolution, justifies the
rule of right no less certainly than an
inadequate science of evolution appears to
justify the rule of force.

Nor, upon examination, have we found
any deep or abiding conflict between those
two branches of the humanitarian movement
which are frequently contrasted under the
names of Liberalism and Socialism.   On

17

the contrary, we find reason for thinking that in ultimate principle both these ideals are at one, and that they have come into conflict only in so far as there has been exaggeration or omission upon one side or upon the other in the way in which the permanent and fundamental conditions of human progress have been conceived. The success of future resistance to the reaction, the possibility of a return to the paths of progress, must depend upon a complete understanding of these two sides of the humanitarian movement. For if our analysis has shown that the ideal of the democratic State is intrinsically sound and necessary to the onward movement of western civilisation—upon the other hand, the bare facts prove that that ideal will not, so to say, act automatically or maintain its supremacy without the most jealous watchfulness on the part of its supporters. Self-government is not in itself a solution of all political and social difficulties. It is at best an instrument with which men who hold by the ideal of social justice and human progress can work, but when those ideals grow cold, it may, like other instruments, be turned to base uses. In the immediate future much will doubtless have to be done towards the perfection of the democratic machine, yet the fundamental reform for which the times call is rather a reconsideration of the ends for which all civilised government exists; in a word, the return to a saner measure of social values. The Liberals of Cobden's day did great things because they had a creed logically reasoned out in relation to the experience of their own time. That creed cannot in its entirety be ours, if only because we have sixty more years of history behind us. But it is only in proportion as we build up a new creed as logical, as sincere, as clearly reasoned out in relation to the experiences of our day, that we shall emerge from the chaos of recent years and present a united front to the forces of reaction. In such a creed self-government will remain a cardinal point, for it is through casting aside self-government that the reaction has made its worst ravages. We shall be under no illusions about democracy. The golden radiance of its morning hopes has long since faded into the light of common day. Yet that dry light of noon serves best for those whose task it is to carry on the work of the world.

APPENDIX

L. T. Hobhouse's Introduction
to the Second Edition

NOTE TO SECOND EDITION

SOME of the more notable changes affecting the argument of this book which have occurred since the publication of the First Edition are briefly referred to here in an Introductory Chapter, in which, by kind permission of the Editor, I have incorporated some pages from an article in the *Contemporary Review* of March, 1908.

INTRODUCTION

FROM the rejection of the Home Rule
Bill in 1886 to the Peace of Vereeniging in 1902 English politics passed through
a period of reaction. It is true that the
long stretch of sixteen years was broken by
three years in which a Liberal Administration held office without power. But the
movement of politics is not to be estimated
by the ebb and flow of party success alone.
It may often be that a party comes into
office only to demonstrate its impotence in
the face of social forces more powerful than
itself; and though General Elections are
one index of opinion, they are not by themselves a sufficient measure of the real
movements of the social tide. The period
of which I speak witnessed an ebb of Liberal
ideas not in this country alone, but throughout the world. It was a time in which the

older conceptions of civil, political and religious liberty lost their vital force; when the middle class, frightened by the first murmurings of Socialism from the cause of progress, and satisfied with the rights which they themselves had won, transferred their influence to the side of established order, when the dominant social philosophy of the day confronted the plea for justice and equality with the doctrine that progress depends on the survival of the stronger in the struggle for existence. The idealism which is essential to modern nations was diverted from the cause of social reform to that of imperial expansion. The white man was bidden to take up as a duty the task which most appealed to his vanity, the task of reducing the millions of the "coloured races" to subjection. Abroad the success of Bismarck had appeared to justify a cynical conception of international duties, and the military, commercial, and political success of a great empire imposed the German ideal on the minds of political thinkers. Across the Atlantic the United States threw off its old traditions like a worn-out garment, em-

braced the Imperial mission, and beginning
a war with an appeal to the sentiment of
humanity, ended it, after the manner of the
Old World, with the acquisition of territory
beyond the seas.

On all sides brute force claimed the justification of success. The Christian Powers,
armed with overwhelming strength, looked
on in helpless impotence at the butchery of
their co-religionists in the Turkish Empire.
The Congo State was fairly launched on its
career of rapine, and through Matabele
wars and Bechuana revolts South Africa
was ripening for its final tragedy. The very
victories won by freedom and nationality in
the previous generation seemed to turn to
dust and nothingness. The French Republic
lay in the grip of the clericals and the
soldiers. Italy paid the penalty of ambition
and aggrandisement, and the outcome of the
enthusiasm of Mazzini and the labours of
Garibaldi seemed to be a people ground
down in poverty beneath the load of a
disgraced and disastrous militarism. It
needed only the farce of the Greek war to
add the touch of ridicule to the discomfiture

of the old Liberal traditions. What wonder if the faith of many waxed cold, and if the new enthusiasm for Empire and order, the machine and the master-mind to work it, found the temples empty, swept, and garnished, and entered undisputed into possession.

To assign dates for the beginning and end of such a movement of reaction is convenient for purposes of reference, but, of course, has no further validity. To seek the beginnings of the ebb of Liberalism we should have to ascend far beyond 1886. Nor can we say distinctly that the tide began to flow again in 1902. British Imperialism, however, received its first check in the South African War, when the course of events opened the eyes of thoughtful people to the inner meaning of the new gospel, and caused them to ask themselves whither it was leading them. The elements of reaction involved in the Imperial idea came more clearly into view. The excitement of the war subsided; and when, in the following year, Mr. Chamberlain launched his scheme of Tariff Reform, the ground was

ready laid for a vigorous resistance. The
Protectionist movement came just too late.
In itself a perfectly logical and natural consequence of the general revolt against the
Liberal idea, it encountered that idea at a
moment when it was gathering fresh strength,
and instead of sweeping it out of existence
only braced it to new life. The more vigorous the attack on the Free Trade system,
the more it revealed its solid foundation in
economic principles and in the hard facts
of British industry. For four years the
Board of Trade figures in their courses
fought against Mr. Chamberlain, and the
movements of industry seemed as though
guided by the Manes of Cobden with the
express object of defeating the predictions
of his critics. People had to admit that at
least in industry freedom had done more
than they had imagined. They had forgotten
its benefits, and it was only when Mr.
Chamberlain compelled them to reopen their
histories that they recalled them. On the
other hand, they now saw unsuspected
dangers in the Imperial union; they began
to reconsider the relation of the mother

country and the colonies, to ask themselves whether the ties of obligation were all on one side, and to criticise the uses to which appeals to colonial sentiment were being put. It was recognised that, after all, industrial and political freedom go together, that the first need in a world-wide empire is that each part should be free to shape its own course, and that if this right was claimed for the dependencies it was paradoxical to deny it to the Motherland. On another side of the field of controversy the vast forces of organised wealth loomed behind the Protectionist attack, and many of those most opposed to Socialistic control awoke to a new sense of the dangers to industrial freedom inherent in the economic structure of modern society. Meanwhile, quite apart from the Free Trade controversy, many causes assisted the Liberal revival. The course of events in South Africa tended to justify the hostile analysis of Imperialism made by those who had been contemptuously dismissed as "pro-Boers." It was recognised that the country could be saved only by the people whom we had spent three years in crushing, that bureaucracy had failed, and that once again there was no salvation but in self-government. At home Nonconformists found that "religious freedom" was no longer a watchword without a meaning, and last, but certainly not least, the world of Labour awoke to the fact that the whole position of trade unionism had been undermined by a series of such decisions as the judicial mind only reaches in periods of general reaction.

The revival was not confined to Great Britain. In the modern world the deeper movements of social opinion can no longer be isolated; but progress and reaction, by their success and failure, propagate waves of encouragement or disillusionment from nation to nation and from continent to continent. The United States has seen to the bottom of its Imperialism, and has learnt to measure if not to grapple with the menace of organised wealth to free institutions. The French Republic has emerged triumphantly from the ordeal of the Dreyfus case, and set its face, not perhaps without some backward looks, in the direction of humanitarian progress. The long night of Russian absolutism itself yielded in 1905 to the first glimmering of a troubled dawn, and Austria, once the centre of European Conservatism, has held her first elections under universal suffrage. In the Far East arose a stranger sign of a new era. The revelation of the power of Japan reacted on Western Europe first by removing from the sphere of aggressive enterprise the vast and seemingly derelict bulk of the Chinese Empire, and, secondly, by unexpectedly proving that the special characteristics of European civilisation are not the privileges of race or colour. Of the full meaning and depth of the impetus given by Japanese example to the people of Asia it is not yet possible to form a decisive opinion. Those who consider the great historic vicissitudes in the relation of the two continents, the alternate domination of one by the thought or by the arms of the other, the slow revivals and gradual but sweeping reversals of position, will be most inclined to see in the new movement in China, India, Turkey, and Persia, the possibility of a gradual but vital change. Those who deny reality to the new phases of Asiatic thought may chasten themselves by reflecting how short is the time since the Japanese adoption of European methods was ascribed to a shallow imitativeness that might be regarded with a tolerant smile. Few thought that the inquiring and intelligent observers who came to Europe to study German discipline and English ships would, in less than a generation, oust Chinese and Russians in succession from Port Arthur, hurl back the tide of Western immigration to the Amur, and shake with the reverberation of their victories the throne of the Tzars.

To see in the movement of the East the signs of a new birth is not to predict its speedy and unbroken triumph in any one quarter. For all we can tell the Young Turks may suffer the fate of the Russian reformers. The Indian bureaucracy may triumph over native "nationalism" and English Liberals. With or without the aid of Cossacks the Shah may prevail at Tabriz. But no succession of reverses can bring back the past when once there has been a loosening of the barriers behind which the spirit of a people has

2

been pent. It is not extravagant to hope that the East has entered on a new career. Hitherto she has given the world all its religions, all its mysticism, half of its philosophy, and much of its romance. But she has sought, not the conquest of nations, but the independence of the spirit in remote kingdoms of its own. When the " younger world " turned upon her,

> " She let the legions thunder past
> Then plunged in thought again."

Now, in a sense which to the author of " Oberman " would have seemed impossible, it is true to write—

> " So well she mused a morning broke
> Across her spirit grey."

The Eastern peoples have, it would seem, learnt from the West one lesson in return for many that they have taught. They have learnt that submission is not the masterword of life. They have learnt from the example of Japan that Europeans have no monopoly of applied science, but that in the mastery of modern industrial processes, in the management of a fleet and the discipline of an army, an Asiatic people can match the world. To argue from the Japanese to the Persian or the Hindoo may, on all ethnological grounds, be the height of absurdity. But we are dealing here, not with a scientific piece of reasoning, but with a psychological force. We are witnessing, so to say, the breakdown of a moral monopoly, and the consequent spreading of an impression among people after people that they can win for themselves the freedom which others enjoy. The process by which this belief is reached is of small moment as compared with the fact that the belief is there. The new hope, the changed attitude, is the datum with which Europe will henceforward have to reckon.

If the change is fraught with immediate anxiety for statesmen it is pregnant with hope for all who take long views of human progress. Until yesterday it was the opinion everywhere prevalent that the East was incapable of self-government, and it is but the other day that popular writers were proving to the general satisfaction, that the function of the West—or rather of one or two chosen peoples of the West—was to "administer" the territories of the Tropics and the East for the general benefit of civilisation. The "sullen new-caught peoples" were to be tamed, if necessary by methods learnt from themselves; the old civilisations were to be quietly guided by blameless civil servants and noiselessly exploited by smiling company promoters. Those who most clearly saw the seamy side of the ideal could hardly resist the analysis of tendency and of fact. Yet, taken at its best and putting aside all consideration of "methods of barbarism" and commercial exploitation, it was a prediction full of grave concern for freedom. Whether the nations that proposed to govern the world could preserve their own freedom in doing so was a question which history inclined us to answer in the negative, and to face it fairly was to admit a grave doubt as to the future of democracy. The awakening of the East has brought a new vision of the future within the limits of possibility. It is conceivable, after all, that to our grandchildren the world will present itself, not as a white

oligarchy, ruling and exploiting unnumbered
millions of yellow, brown, and black, but as
a system of self-governing peoples linked
by mutual respect and international agree-
ment rather than by bonds of authority and
subordination. To prophesy in this sense
would doubtless be premature. The East,
which for our purpose extends from the
Japanese Empire to the Austrian frontier, has
yet to prove its capacity for the self-government which it claims. Yet in this matter
statesmen and thinkers have generally agreed
that the claim itself, if genuine, is the first,
and in the absence of experience the best,
proof that can be given of competence. That
men may be able to govern themselves the
prime condition is that they should genuinely
desire to do so. Given this desire, given a
definite type of civilisation that has become
conscious of its own value and is sensibly
irritated and confined by the pressure of an
alien government, and we have ready to hand
the realities on which national freedom may
rest, as distinct from the rhetoric and the
formulæ that an educated class may pick up
at University lectures. Sociologists are ac-

customed to speak of the relativity of institutions. They insist, in particular, that it may be disastrous to equip a backward people with a political order embodying the highest known ideals of social justice. Such ideals, they say, are to be reached only by a slow process of development, and we shall merely do harm if we impose them on a people that is not ready for them. The reasoning is just, but on its own suppositions it ceases to apply when the conception of a higher order has once begun to take hold of a race. From that time forward the work of the progressive statesman is to cultivate the new spirit even while it doubles the difficulties of government. Such is the situation with which our own Indian administration is confronted. It has not now to deal with academics but with realities. We have no longer to talk of applying Western ideals to Indian life : we have rather to open channels of practical efficacy into which ideals that India has made her own can flow unimpeded by her internal diversities or by her relation to the British Crown. Such a task in such circumstances is the supreme test of statesmanship and the touchstone of Liberal principle. Fortune has dealt fairly by us in entrusting it to the greatest living disciple of Mill and Gladstone.

Thus the events of the four years which have passed since the following chapters were printed have deeply affected the problems with which they deal. On the principal question raised, the future of democracy, they have shed a new and hopeful light. Of the practical problems of British politics to which reference was made, some have been solved with a success surpassing expectation by the application of well-known Liberal principles. Others, unfortunately, are no farther advanced than before. White South Africa, for example, has definitely won its freedom, and the principle of self-government is displaying to the full its power of over-coming divergences and reconciling animosities which outside interference could only embitter ; on the other hand, the problem of the aboriginal population is no nearer a solution than of old, and in the tangle of human affairs the principle of autonomy is itself invoked in defence of the unlimited right of a little oligarchy of planters to deal as they please with the black man within their gates. The action of Natal in the past three years would have afforded, had she been a South African Republic rich in gold, a score of *casus belli* to a beneficent Empire. But precisely because she is our own colony we are bound hand and foot in dealing with her. She claims the unrestricted right to "larrup her own niggers," and enforces it both literally and metaphorically without the slightest regard to the traditions of British law or the representations of an Imperial Government to which she has ever boasted her especial loyalty. In part, her attitude is a *sequela* of the worst days of Imperialism. The impression first engendered during the South African War and deepened in the Tariff Reform campaign, that the mother country was under a positive obligation to the colonies for condescending to remain under her protection, and would go cap in hand to them to execute their smallest desires, has seriously impaired the authority of the Imperial Government and shaken the moral solidarity of the Empire. Natal has been told, in effect, that she may flaunt us as she chooses—and she does choose. At the same time, some of our own dealings in South Africa are too recent to admit of our intervening as a nation with moral effect on behalf of justice to a weaker race. We approach the native problem in the moment of South African unification with one hand tied behind us. Yet if there is any question of the internal politics of a colony on which the Home Government has a right to be heard, it is that of the unrepresented native. We have given what is called self-government to the South African colonies. More strictly, we have given the white races the power to govern themselves and the black, to say nothing of excluding our own fellow-subjects from other parts of the Empire if they choose. If the Imperial connection has any meaning at all, it should appear when the rights of the native are in question. This is not to impair the principle of self-government, for, except in Cape Colony, there is no self-government where the Bantu races are concerned. It is merely to recognise a certain measure of responsibility for those whom we have chosen by our own act to make subjects of the

British Crown. Is it too much to hope that South African statesmen, who have measured by bitter experience the extent of the difference between government by authority and government by consent, will set themselves resolutely to overcome racial prejudice and to settle South African freedom on the broad basis of enfranchisement, irrespective of colour, for all who accept the essentials of civilised life?

In our domestic politics the electoral revolution of 1906 might at first sight be taken as a decisive reassertion of democratic ideas. It is true that it continued and emphasised the public protest against certain features of the reaction, the beginnings of which were already noticeable when the following chapters were first printed. But in reality General Elections determine less than appears. They decide who shall govern the country, but not how it shall be governed. The great machine rolls on, guided by civil servants, judges, magistrates, borough councils, and the first lesson incoming ministers learn is the narrow limitation of their power. If we ask how far the Liberal and Labour parties have succeeded in inspiring the actual conduct of affairs with their spirit and in revitalising democracy, the answer cannot be given with any confidence. Much has been attempted and something done. But some ominous tendencies stand out. In spite, or even in consequence, of a Liberal House of Commons the hereditary principle has steadily increased its influence. The House of Lords has hitherto gained ground in every encounter with the House of Commons. This is no mere accident. It is not due solely to the skilful leading of the Peers or to the divided and distracted counsels of the Government. It is the reflection of the actual power of the great material interests, which, though temporarily beaten at the polls, have great and growing forces at their back. They have " society " as their permanent defender. They have now almost the whole Press, which is definitely ceasing to be a representative organ of public opinion. They have the power of the purse, which, as expenses multiply and the scale of operations is enlarged, becomes more and more the controlling factor in political education and agitation. If these forces control the House of Commons, they have no need of a second chamber; if for a moment they lose control, then the Upper House is ready to hand as their constitutional instrument. Without them the Lords would be powerless. Without the Lords they would have no means, within the Constitution, of defeating the expressed will of the people. As things stand, unless the next twelve months should show an unexpected change, these forces bid fair to prove to British democracy that it cannot get its will effected except so far as they consent. They are not strong enough to avoid concessions, but on the record of the past three years they appear strong enough to destroy government by the majority and to frustrate the representative House.

Meanwhile the hereditary principle has shown unexpected strength in another direction. This is not the place for a discussion of the new position of the Sovereign in public affairs. But the briefest note on contemporary political tendency cannot omit the silent revolution effected by the present

King. How far the revolution has gone is, indeed, one of the questions on which light is desirable. What precisely is the division of responsibility between the King and the Foreign Secretary, and how continuity of policy is maintained under the new system, are questions which will some day have to be answered. I do not propose to offer conjectural solutions, nor to enter at present into an examination of the spirit in which our foreign policy is being conducted. I note only the constitutional change whereby the monarchy has abandoned the position which it had come to occupy in the minds of the people as the representative and embodiment of the nation placed above the controversies over which it presided. In taking an overt part in the direction of policy the Sovereign is necessarily brought within the sphere of political debate. Questions arise of the use of the social influence of the Court in politics. The King's authority is quoted on this side and that, and the main constitutional understanding on which the monarchy rests is threatened. These changes are accepted with that supineness which continues to characterise the public in all matters that seriously affect its permanent welfare, and must form a serious item in the account when we are balancing the gains and losses of the democratic principle.

On the other side of the account must be set the revival in no stinted measure of the old feeling for social progress and for political freedom. The movement for the enfranchisement of women is prominent among the evidences of a revival of the democratic spirit, and it is one of the paradoxes which throw light on the inner connection of political ideas that this movement finds organised support in the party which was wont to justify its independence of Liberalism on the ground that the work of political emancipation was substantially complete and that the time had arrived for concentration on social progress. The truth is that political progress is never complete in one direction while it lags behind in others. But be this as it may, the feeling for liberty and the feeling for social justice are equally alive in the public life of the present day.

Such feeling would, indeed, be the governing force in politics if it could do justice to itself in practical expression. But it is one thing for men to feel strongly on social matters and quite another to arrive at a coherent plan of reform which will bind together in action the easily estranged forces of thin-skinned and irritable idealists. There is a certain social idealism common to many schools of reformers, but there exists no creed in which its doctrines are embodied with such authority as to command general assent, to lay out a plan of campaign, and to dictate the order in which different reforms are to be approached. Hence a disastrous loss of energy; hence the endless divisions and recriminations between those who are at bottom for the same end, and who, if they thoroughly understood one another, would realise that they were allied in spirit against the Philistine.

The distraction may be measured in the political conditions which reflect it. The old English party system is undermined. Though not yet replaced by the group system of organisation familiar to the Continent, it is honeycombed by what may be called group opinions. The members of a large set of groups call themselves collectively Liberals, and acquiesce with greater or less heartiness in the orthodox Liberal creed. But in reality each is far more intent on its sectional ends than on general measures for the realisation of a distinct democratic ideal. People are Temperance Reformers, Woman Suffragists, Land Taxers, Big Navy Men, Economists, and so forth before they are Liberals. Their effective work is given to advancing the interests of their group; and there is more joy over a resolution which is held to pledge the party to some pet point, which, after all, may never see the inside of the Statute Book, than over the successful passage into law of a measure commanding the assent of the party as a whole. There is no cohesion in the democratic crew, no whole-hearted general backing for the measures which the enthusiasm of a group imposes on a somewhat reluctant party.

It is true that along one particular line of divergences the cleavage is represented

by a distinct organisation. It may be urged
that in the mind of the Labour Party at
least we have a social ideal, which we may
like or dislike, but which we must admit
to be coherent, comprehensive, and logical.
But in reality the position of the Labour
Party is one of the paradoxes of politics.
To begin with, the cleavage which it makes
does not correspond with the real fissure of
opinion. There is no division in principle
or method between its main body and the
advanced Liberals. The ideas of Socialism,
when translated into practical terms, coincide
with the ideas to which Liberals are led when
they seek to apply their principles of Liberty,
Equality, and the Common Good to the
industrial life of our time. Within the
Labour Party there is a real division between the doctrinaire Socialism, which is
concerned primarily with the academic
assertion of ideals, and the practical collectivism of the Trade Union leaders. Within
the Liberal Party there is a real and deep
division between the men who are for
developing and expanding the Radical tradition and those who regard Liberalism as

the more enlightened method of maintaining the existing social order. But these lines of cleavage, which appear in every measure of legislation and every act of policy, cut across the division of the two parties. The party tie holds together men who are in essentials opposed, and divides those who in spirit are agreed.

That Liberalism and Socialism move on converging lines, or, if the expression be preferred, that they represent complementary and mutually necessary aspects of the social ideal, is by no means universally admitted on either side. The argument by which I endeavoured to justify this view in the present work was, I admit, all too brief. In his generous appreciation of this volume as a whole, Lord Morley has with perfect justice demanded a far deeper and more thorough-going analysis. If I have let the chapter remain without alteration or supplement, it is not that I ignore the weight of this criticism, but because I feel it impossible to do justice to the subject in less than a volume. That freedom and mutual aid are the twin foundations of social life, that the ideas belonging to them are complementary and not exclusive, that historically the one side has been developed sometimes with too narrow an interpretation by Liberalism and the other by Socialism, are opinions which I firmly hold, but which I cannot fruitfully elaborate further than has already been done without exceeding the limits of the present work. For the moment, therefore, I leave the argument where it stood.

The common ground on which Liberals and Socialists are believed to stand has been spoken of as Social Idealism. The term might seem to connect the writer with the idealism of metaphysics, and a word should therefore be said on the repudiation of metaphysical idealism in the body of the work. In the opinion of a valued critic, Professor H. Jones, I have been less than just to the philosophy of which he is a distinguished exponent. In suggesting that the effect of idealistic teaching on ordinary people has been on the whole to " soften the edges of all hard contrasts between right and wrong," I have missed, in his opinion, the essence of its philosophy. Like other critics of idealism, I fail because I insist on "exclusive" assumptions. For me, for example, either evil is real and, if so, the world is imperfect, or the world order is perfect and, if so, the appearance of evil is appearance only. Idealism repudiates such alternatives. It maintains, in Professor Jones's words, "an irrefragable optimism to which

'The evil is null, is nought, is silence, implying sound,'

and side by side with that trust a deep conviction of the terrible reality of sin." Those who, like myself, remain incapable of combining these views, will, like myself, remain of opinion that the one must tend to destroy the other, and that the profounder the conviction that the world order is perfect the easier accordingly will be the acquiescence in the prevailing tendency of the time. If all that is real is rational, it is difficult to resist the view that what wins is right.

Professor Jones takes strong exception in particular to my ascription to idealism of the view that "every institution and every belief is alike a manifestation of a spiritual principle."

All are spiritual but not equally spiritual. His reply is just, so far as it calls attention to the attempts of idealists to distinguish degrees or orders of truth and of reality in their system. But on my side I may be allowed to point to the dissatisfaction—the very creditable dissatisfaction—of the idealists themselves with this side of their theory. T. H. Green, for example, himself criticises the Hegelian theory of the State precisely for its want of discrimination between different degrees in the realisation of the ideal :—

"To an Athenian slave, who might be used to gratify a master's lust, it would have been a mockery to speak of the State as a realisation of freedom ; and perhaps it would not be much less so to speak of it as such to an untaught and underfed denizen of a London yard with ginshops on the right hand and on the left. What Hegel says of the State in this respect seems as hard to square with facts as what St. Paul says of the Christian whom the manifestation of Christ has transferred from bondage into "the glorious liberty of the sons of God." In both cases the difference between the ideal and the actual seems to be ignored, and tendencies seem to be spoken of as if they were accomplished facts. . . . Hegel's account of freedom as realised in the State does not seem to correspond to the facts of society as it is, or even as, under the unalterable conditions of human nature, it ever could be : though undoubtedly there is a work of moral liberation which society, through its various agencies, is constantly carrying on for the individual." *

As a teacher and reformer Green himself was thoroughly alive to "the difference between the ideal and the actual." Yet his metaphysical theory supplies no adequate explanation of the gulf between them. The failure, I would venture to maintain, is inherent in idealism. To realise the tragedy of human life and history, to feel within oneself some pale reflex of the massive suffering of millions, to sound the abysses of woe and despair that ring round the securest life, to be possessed of this vision of blackness, and at the same moment to proclaim that "the earth is the Lord's, and the fulness thereof," nay, that all that we have seen has its being in a Spirit that is perfect—that is what I cannot do. It is what I suspect no one can do. It is more likely that those who think they do pass from one view to the other and mean less by the terms in which they seek to reconcile them than they suppose. †

* "The Sense of Freedom in Morality" ("Works," vol. ii., p. 314).

† It is right, however, to say that I have on revision

Professor Jones reproves me also for generalising overmuch. He finds what I say about the temper of the time true in part but greatly exaggerated as a picture of the generation as a whole, an exaggeration which he finds excusable only by the date—shortly after the close of the South African War—at which the book was written. I fear I may incur a deeper censure by reprinting it in this "cool and calm hour" with but few alterations. An explanation is certainly due to the reader on this point. The book was an attempt to characterise in broad outline the thought and feeling, the prevailing temper and dominant tone, of a period. So far as it is an indictment, it is directed, not against a party, nor yet—and it is here that Professor Jones, I think, misinterprets it—against a nation. It is an indictment of a mood, which for a time dominated public life, of tendencies engendering that mood and arguments brought to justify it. The mood is no longer dominant,

modified some sentences which appear to do less than justice to the elements of positive value contributed by Idealism to social ethics.

INTRODUCTION

but the tendencies and arguments associated with it are abiding, though for a while less influential, factors in public life. If, therefore, the delineation had any value at all, the value is permanent, and it would be destroyed by corrections bringing it "up to date," by the use of illustrations drawn from the present instead of those which suggested themselves at the time of writing. I have, therefore, left such references substantially unchanged, noting only when it seemed necessary such events as have closely affected the matters referred to. My object was to attempt a brief delineation of Imperialism, and in this I cannot find after four years that I have anything substantial to withdraw. My object was also to point out certain weaknesses in democratic government and certain dangers to liberty, and though new grounds of hope have appeared, the weaknesses and dangers remain. The hot fit of Imperialism is past, but the cold fit succeeds. Those who the other day were loudest in proclaiming their nation the appointed rulers of mankind are now in panic because our neighbours want to have one warship to our two. The same press influences which so misled the nation in the matter of South Africa can proceed seemingly with undiminished influence to work up a scare on the subject of Germany. The methods used are substantially the same, except that the appeal is no longer to vainglory or to vindictiveness, but to fear. The same arts working on the same emotional credulity create the same atmosphere of suspicion, and the whole rests on the same psychological basis—the refusal of people to measure foreigners coolly as men moved by emotions like their own, governed by like fears, and ready to listen to like arguments. The mob mind has forgotten everything and learnt nothing, and the danger inherent in the permanent presence of this mass of inflammable material has in no sense passed away. The warfare with such tendencies is not one that ends at a stroke with victory or defeat. It renews itself in an endless variety of forms, and each campaign has a lesson of permanent value for those who will learn. But to recognise the continuance of the struggle is not to despair of the result. It would be sheer pessimism to refuse to see the brighter outlook which the last few years have brought the world as a whole. Freedom has shown its recuperative power, and the better elements of opinion tend to more organic shape. The grounds of fear for the future of democracy have not vanished, but the grounds of hope have been consolidated and enlarged.

Notes to the Text

1. p.6. 1.29.
Free Trade and other fundamental doctrines of the Manchester School, set forth in selections from the speeches and writings of its founders and followers, edited and with an introduction by F.W. Hirst (1903).

2. p.16. 1.8. to p.29 1.9.
This is a much expanded version of the article in the *Speaker*, 18 January 1902.

3. p.17. 1.14
A great Imperialist. In the *Speaker* this reference was explicitly to Joseph Chamberlain.

4. p.19. 1.12.
merely a burden. In the *Speaker* Hobhouse continued: "That was an argument which appealed to men like Bentham, and from the time of the American war onwards" etc. This, therefore, is the context for the reference to Bentham on p.20.

5. pp.20-3.
The concrete illustration of the Radical attitude to Empire did not appear in the *Speaker*.

6. p.22. 1.23.
John Morley, *The Life of Richard Cobden* (1881).

7. p.23. 1.26.
John Morley, *The Life of William Ewart Gladstone* (1903).

8. p.24. 1.8 to p.25 1.11.
This passage is also new. It is clearly aimed at Chamberlain.

9. pp.26-7.
The treatment of India here is less anti-imperialist than that of its original in the *Speaker*. The possibility should not be ruled out that Hobhouse's uncle, Lord Hobhouse, with his long experience of British rule in India, may have been responsible for this amendment. We know from the prefatory Note that he made suggestions about the manuscript.

10. pp. 35-6
The remarks about Chinese labour in South Africa were omitted from the second edition.

11. p.38. l.25.
Kanaka traffic, i.e. the importation of Pacific Islanders into Australia as cheap labour.

12. p.39. l.15.
Sir Godfrey Lagden, Commissioner for Native Affairs in South Africa, 1901-7.

13. pp.42. ff.
The references to South Africa were updated in the second edition, and the assertion was made that Liberal policy there had been vindicated.

14. p.43. l.22.
Tarbutt, Cresswell. F.H.W. Cresswell was one of the few mine managers to campaign for white labour in South Africa and was responsible for publicising correspondence such as this.

15. p.47. l.6.
The rest of this paragraph is loosely based on the *Speaker,* 18 January 1902.

16. p.52.
Hobhouse has in mind here the Workmen's Compensation Act of 1897; the Education Act of 1902; and the Licensing Act of 1904. The last two provoked fierce Liberal opposition.

17. p.57. l.10 to p. 62 l.19.
This passage closely follows the *Speaker,* 1 February 1902.

18. p.61. l.7.
A.E.M. Ashley, *The Life of H.J. Temple, Viscount Palmerston, 1846-1865* (1876).

19. p.61. l.9.
Hardinge's despatches. Hardinge had formerly been Consul General in East Africa.

20. p.63. l.19 to p.67 l.21.
The quotation here is from the *Speaker,* 8 February 1902.

21. p.65. l.14.
John Morley *The Life of Richard Cobden* (1881)

22. p.66. l.15.
at home. This was followed in the original by a reference to Hobson's

Speaker articles and an assertion that events in South Africa illustrated the point.

23. p.77. 1.17 to p. 80 1.2.
From the *Speaker*, 8 February 1902.

24. p.78. 1.20.
In the second edition the criticism of Idealism is softened at this point.

25. p.81 n.
Hobhouse was clearly impressed with the force of this article, which is apparently the basis of his reference to Clarke in *The Metaphysical Theory of the State*, p.24.

26. p.84. 1.10 to p.87. 1.21.
This passage is based on the *Speaker*, 1 February 1902.

27. p.114. 1.18.
Karl Pearson. Professor of Mathematics at University College London and a leading exponent of 'Social Darwinism'. The reference is to his *National Life from the standpoint of Science* (1900).

28. p.120. 1.4.
The discussion of "the expert" originally followed on from the argument now concluded at p. 151 1.4.

29. p.122. 1.26.
Theodor Mommsen, *The History of Rome*, English translation (1862-75).

30. p.137.
In the second edition Hobhouse noted that the questions raised in ch.5 are explored further in his *Morals in Evolution*, vol.ii, ch.7.

31. pp.138-9.
In the second edition the test questions for democracy are reformulated in a sense taking account of the Liberal election victory in 1906.

32. p.139. 1.3 to p.147. 1.19.
This passage follows the *Speaker*, 28 December 1901.

33. p.147. 1.20 to p.157 1.6.
This passage follows the *Speaker*, 4 January 1902.

34. p.153. 1.26 to p.155. 1.14.
Hobhouse's original version was a more enthusiastic commendation of federalism as a solution to Imperial problems. At the same time, the original included a more explicit criticism of Milner's policy at this point.

35. p. 157. 1.7 to p.164. 1.23.
This passage is based on the *Speaker*, 11 January 1902.

36. p.158. 1.6.
Whiteley's, synonymous with a large chain-store.

37. p.159. 1.10.
Messrs. Wernher, Beit and Co. The most famous of the Rand mining companies, not least because it lent itself to anti-semitic smears.

38. p.159. 1.16.
In the *Speaker* version there was a footnote at this point quoting from, and taking issue with, the arguments in *Fabianism and the Empire*, by George Bernard Shaw (1900), pp.22 ff.

39. p.168. 1.1 to p.180. 1.8.
This passage follows the *Speaker*, 25 January 1902.

40. p.168. 1.20.
govern themselves. In the original this runs straight on to "It is not democratic self-government" etc. (p.169. 1.20). The intervening paragraph is thus quite new.

41. p.170. 1.27.
The Works of Jeremy Bentham edited by John Bowring, first published in 1843.

42. p.170 n.
The quotation from Bentham has been added subsequently; and the same is true at p.172. 1.11 and p.174. 1.11.

43. p.171. 1.27.
James Legge, *Confucian Analects, the Great Learning, the Doctrine of the Mean*, first published in London, 1861.

44. p.175. 1.24.
Courtney. Leonard Courtney (later Lord Courtney of Penwith) was practically the only well-known Unionist to oppose the War.

45. p.176. 1.19.
the things done in his name. This was originally an explicit reference to the Borneo massacres.

46. p.179. 1.14.
Disraeli's first lieutenant, i.e. Salisbury.

47. p.203 n.
In the second edition Hobhouse added here a laudatory reference to the Young Turks.

48. p.206. 11. 14, 15, 16.
Ionian Islands, Alabama arbitration, Pretoria Convention. The cession of the Ionian Islands to Greece (1863), the acceptance of arbitration over the United States Government's claims against the *Alabama* (1872), and the grant of independence to the Transvaal by the Pretoria Convention (1882), were all examples of a 'Gladstonian' approach to foreign policy – though Gladstone at the time opposed the first of these.

49. p.206. 1.20.
Thibet. The British Government was at this time much exercised over Russian designs on Tibet. The Younghusband mission of 1904-5 successfully re-established British influence without annexation. Hobhouse's fears were to this extent proved groundless and the footnote was excised from the second edition.

50. p.226. 1.26.
John Stuart Mill, *Autobiography* (1873).

51. p.232. 1.14.
the last great Liberal Budget. Harcourt's Budget of 1894, which introduced death duties.

52. p.236. 1.23.
Thomas Kirkup, *A History of Socialism* (1892): 4th edition (1909), 226-8, 228-9.

Bibliography

Among Hobhouse's other works of political theory those most closely related to *Democracy and Reaction* are:

The Labour Movement, with a preface by R.B. Haldane, T. Fisher Unwin, 1893 of which there were several subsequent editions;

Liberalism, Home University Library, 1911, which was in print for many years and has since been published in a Galaxy Books edition with an introduction by Alan P. Grimes, New York, Oxford University Press, 1964;

Social Evolution and Political Theory, New York, Columbia University Press, 1911, the lectures Hobhouse gave in America. This volume is still available.

Two of his academic studies can be regarded as contemporary with *Democracy and Reaction*:

Mind in Evolution, Macmillan, 1901;

Morals in Evolution: a study in comparative ethics (Chapman and Hall, 1906) to the seventh edition of which (1951) Morris Ginsberg contributed an introduction.

The other full-scale scholarly work which has a bearing here is:

The Metaphysical Theory of the State: a criticism, George Allen and Unwin, 1918.

The centenary volume of articles and essays, *Sociology and Philosophy*, edited by Morris Ginsberg, G. Bell for the London School of Economics, 1966, reprints three of the shorter works cited above, *viz:*

'The historical evolution of property, in fact and in idea' from *Property: its rights and duties*, introduced by Charles Gore, Macmillan, 1913;

'The philosophy of development' from *Contemporary British Philosophy*, edited by J.H. Muirhead, George Allen and Unwin, 1924;

The Roots of Modern Sociology, University of London, 1908, Hobhouse's inaugural lecture.

Of Hobhouse's ephemera – considerable in itself – one pamphlet deserves special notice here:

Government by the People, The People's Suffrage Federation, 1910.

There are, too, his numerous contributions, signed and unsigned, to the *Manchester Guardian,* some of which were reprinted in:

L.T. Hobhouse, His life and work, by J.A. Hobson and Morris Ginsberg, George Allen and Unwin, 1931. This is the best single account of his life.

The important relationship with C.P. Scott is also illuminated in three works: J.L. Hammond, *C.P. Scott of the 'Manchester Guardian',* G. Bell, 1934.

C.P. Scott, 1846-1932. The Making of the 'Manchester Guardian', Frederick Muller, 1946;

Trevor Wilson (ed.), *The Political Diaries of C.P. Scott, 1911-1928,* Collins 1970.

The progressive critique of Imperialism is ably examined in:

Bernard Porter, *Critics of Empire, British radical attitudes to colonialism in Africa, 1895-1914,* Macmillan, 1968.

The electoral politics of 'the progressive era' are analysed in:

P.F. Clarke, *Lancashire and the New Liberalism,* Cambridge University Press, 1971.

Hobhouse's place in the evolution of Liberalism is suggested in:

Alan Bullock and Maurice Shock, *The Liberal Tradition, from Fox to Keynes,* A. & C. Black, 1956.

There is an interesting examination of Green in:

Melvin Richter, *The Politics of Conscience. T.H. Green and His Age,* Weidenfeld and Nicolson, 1964, which corrects some of the misconceptions in:

H.J. Laski, *The Decline of Liberalism,* Hobhouse Memorial Trust Lecture, Oxford University Press, 1940.

The evolutionary context of Hobhouse's thought is touched on perceptively in:

J.W. Burrow, *Evolution and Society,* Cambridge University Press, 1966; second edition, 1970.